FITNESS AND FIGURE CONTROL: THE CREATION OF YOU

LINDA GARRISON
PHYLLIS LESLIE
DEBORAH BLACKMORE
Mt. San Antonio College

Mayfield Publishing Company

This book is dedicated to our staff,
students, college, and community—the
people who made a dream come true.

Library of Congress Catalog Card Number:
74-84565
International Standard Book Number:
0-87484-246-8 (paper)

Manufactured in the United States of America

Mayfield Publishing Company
285 Hamilton Avenue
Palo Alto, California 94301

Poem on page 7 from *The Poetry of Robert
Frost* edited by Edward Connery Lathem.
Copyright 1916, ©1969 by Holt, Rinehart,
and Winston, Inc. Copyright 1944 by Robert
Frost. Reprinted by permission of Holt,
Rinehart and Winston, Inc. Epigraph on page
89 from *My Gift to You* by George Betts.
Millbrae, Calif.: Celestial Arts, 1972. Epi-
graph on page 90 from *This Time Called Life*
by Walter Rinder. Millbrae, Calif.: Celestial
Arts, 1971. Used by permission.

Thanks to CSC Athletic Equipment of San
Pedro, California, for assembling illustrations
of the larger pieces of gym equipment.

CONTENTS

APPENDIX: CHARTS   91

PRELUDE

*Only those who have already experienced
a revolution within themselves can reach
out effectively to help others.*

— Malcolm X

We believe in life! It is a challenge to exist in today's world, to be sure, but what a wonderful challenge! When there is harmony between mind and body, when you are in touch with yourself as an individual and awakened to your own creative potential, you discover a zest for living that burns brighter every day. That is the lesson exercise has taught us—that, and the remarkable truth that *in shaping your figure you can learn how to shape your life.* Quite a discovery, you'll agree, and we are eager to share it with you.

That is why this is more than just a book on exercise. It is designed to help you begin working on that person deep inside you so that you can set your individualism free and meet each day with a full charge of positive energy. You see, we *know* you can learn to delight in each breath you draw, to move with joy through a life lived to its fullest, and to see each day of that life as a shining new challenge.

You are unique in all the world. Become aware of that—aware of yourself as a special combination of capabilities and attitudes and feelings contained in a body that is one of a kind, and endowed with a life that has never been lived before. Pack each day full of new ideas and new experiences, and do as much as time will allow. Avoid self-pity or self-neglect. Make action and readiness a part of your life. In the words of Erich Fromm, "Those whose hope is strong see and cherish all signs of life and are ready every moment to help that which is ready to be born."

Life is what you make it. And you *can* make it! Remember this as you follow our exercise plan, and you will be successful.

L.G.
P.L.
D.B.

ACKNOWLEDGMENTS

The authors wish to thank John Cates of the University of California, San Diego; George Dehnel of the College of San Mateo; Ann Read of Fullerton College; and Jack Wilmore of the University of California, Davis, who read the manuscript in its development stages and offered valuable suggestions that were incorporated into the finished product.

Be it remembered that until woman comes to her kingdom physically, she will never really come at all. Created to be well and strong and beautiful, she long ago sacrificed her constitution. She has walked when she should have run, sat when she should have walked, reclined when she should have sat. She is a creature born to beauty and freedom.

—Edward Bellamy

THE BEGINNING

The past is but the beginning of a
beginning, and all that is and has been
is but the twilight of the dawn.

— H. G. Wells

Walk on beyond, leave the past behind.
Discover yourself as you are now.

— George Betts

YOU AND YOUR WORLD

Life in the last half of the twentieth century has become hectic and fast-moving.
It is difficult to comprehend how highly developed and complex our society has
become. We stand in witness to an awesome man-made technology and the
constant change it imposes upon our world. Some of us view this change with
optimism and enthusiasm—each day bringing new discoveries, insights, and
improvements. Others view it with apprehension, fearful of losing the wisdom of
the past in the glitter of today and the bright glow of the future.

1

It has always been difficult to register the impact of "progress" on the human being. Thus far we have shown a certain ability to adapt to progress, but how well and for how long? Somewhere between the infinity of the universe and the complexity of the molecule lie the limits of our abilities. It will take courage and stamina to explore these limits. Meanwhile, we search for a life-style combining new-found knowledge and self-awareness with the value of past wisdoms.

A good beginning is to accept the interrelationship of mind and body. Each contributes in the total effort of living life to its fullest. There is no isolation in the development of the complete person, only a balance of intertwining variables. An awareness of the potential and needs of each aspect of your personality—intellectual, emotional, spiritual, and physical—is necessary to your personal growth as well as to your successes in life.

You must understand that you control your own successes and achievements by determining your individual life-style. Let us hope you will choose a life-style that leads to the development of the total human being. Our life-styles are created out of the attitudes with which we face life. If you are looking for a prosperous, satisfying life, you must develop your ability to adapt to change.

We stress this development because, ironically, change has become the most permanent condition of modern living. What effect this condition will have on human cultural evolution remains in question. Nor can we foresee what our current fascination with modern convenience will cost us in terms of the development of human potential. As we rely more on the ease of living provided by technology, we find ourselves faced with a growing number of health problems stemming from the neglect of our physical bodies. In America today, obesity is a health problem of epidemic proportions, and heart disease is now the most frequent cause of death. Technology has created a tremendous void, for the daily routine of living does not include enough activity to tax us physically or to make positive use of the amounts of food we consume.

When we finally began to acknowledge an energy crisis in the world, we realized how dependent upon mechanical energy our way of living has become. A growing sensitivity to the sources and use of energy has indeed developed, but we must see that this sensitivity continues. We must always remain aware of the cost of technology in terms of our physical beings. To be able to sit and watch television is fine, but we must be constantly aware of what will happen if we do not plan activities to counteract the time we spend sitting. If we are to reap the rewards that life has to offer, we must learn to use the advances of technology wisely, and must keep in mind the importance of daily physical exercise and dietary habits that correspond to physical demands.

YOU IN SEARCH OF SELF

Today's woman has been deeply affected by recent social change. Woman's potential now seems infinitely greater than we ever dared to hope. It is with excitement that we are discovering ourselves as whole human beings and recognizing that women's goals need no longer be proscribed by traditional definitions of femininity. The door is opening for us to use whatever ambitions and talents we possess.

A realistic perception of self in terms of attitudes, needs, aspirations, and capabilities is a necessary accomplishment in learning to live effectively. The woman emerging on the modern scene emphasizes her individual strengths and expresses her personal values in a much broader sense than ever before. It will take courage and conviction to assume a new identity and accept the accompanying responsibilities. The demands on women in our society are being intensified, and we must be physically ready to live with the pressures they will bring.

Regardless of the particular path or paths you've chosen—student, wife, mother, career woman, or adventurer—you must realize that modern technology has limited, to a great degree, your world of physical experience. Lack of physical activity is one of the reasons women have problems in maintaining health and figure. The task is not an easy one for any of us!

Take the case of the student, whether she is a girl in her teens or a woman returning to college after many years. The mental tasks of learning do not burn many calories. One of the most difficult tasks is learning to balance food intake and activity when priority must be given to studies, when many hours must be spent quietly listening, reading, and writing. Many students find that the pressure of deadlines and exams causes them to nibble on snacks or to over-eat. These are habits which can be controlled. One of the hazards of dormitory life can be the starchy foods served in the campus dining commons. The dorm student must learn to select her food carefully. Incidentally, several campus cafeterias and snack bars have recognized this problem and are now providing special low-calorie meals.

The woman running a household usually assumes the major responsibility of feeding her family. With food at her fingertips much of the time, she must develop strong will power to resist the temptation to snack. This is not a superhuman task; it is merely hard work. Because men and growing children burn calories at a faster rate than most women, their food needs are greater.[1] This fact is a source of frustration for women who cannot accept the limits they must place on their own diet. Most household jobs consist of small movements which don't burn many calories, even though they may seem exhausting. For instance, cooking, washing dishes, and dusting have been calculated at using only two to three calories per minute.[2] In a well-designed home equipped with refrig-

[1] Sue Rodwell Williams, *Nutrition and Diet Therapy* (Saint Louis: The C. V. Mosby Company, 1969), p. 68.
[2] L. Jean Bogert, George M. Briggs, and Doris H. Calloway, *Nutrition and Physical Fitness* (Philadelphia: W. B. Saunders Company, 1973) p. 40.

erator, washer, dryer, and vacuum cleaner, the task of housework can no longer be considered a physically taxing job. The fatigue many housewives experience comes less from physical exertion than from the frustrations and fragmentation of a daily routine of chores; necessary jobs, to be sure, but not worth accomplishing at the expense of self! Time and a place for rest and creative interests must be a part of each woman's life in order to rejuvenate her own mind and body.

The career woman may also tend to neglect her own needs. Bound and determined to subsist independently, she may leave little time and energy at the end of each working day for preparing proper meals, let alone for physical activity and exercise. Weekends are precious, saved for shopping excursions and errands she didn't find time for during the week. Yet today's working woman must compensate for her hours of inactivity and her use on the job of such energy-saving devices as electric typewriters, calculators, collators, computers, and automatic duplicating machines instead of the old manually operated equipment. For instance, if she changes from a manual to an electric typewriter she can add as much as four pounds per year in burning fewer calories, provided all other factors remain the same. In ten years she could gain forty pounds!

Just being born female, in our culture, has added the disadvantage of an upbringing and environment which limits our physical activity and, as a result, our confidence about physical pursuits. In the past, boys have been taught to be active while girls have been taught to be passive and have not been taught respect for their physical strengths and needs. Few experiences reinforcing the concept of active living have been provided for girls. Yet the attitudes necessary to motivate us throughout our lifetime are the result of early childhood experiences. Thus, we can understand why many women do not identify with, or even clearly perceive, the physical experience of living. Susan Edminston, in an article explaining the growing awareness among women of a more active type of living, has written: "There is a shift of perspective that takes place, a shift from doing things *to* your body—painting, clothing or starving it—to doing things *with* it, and a corresponding change from passivity to activity."[3] We can sit back and accept life the way it has been handed to us, or we can assume the task of directing our lives toward the goals we choose. The figure we desire and are capable of having will not just happen. There are no fairy godmothers in the real world to wave their magic wands and make us instantly slim and beautiful. But there is a very real and powerful force deep within each one of us, if we will only take the time to find it and cultivate it. The discipline of will power and the force of self-respect exist in all of us, simply waiting to be set free.

---

[3] Susan Edminston, "The Gymsuit Blues; Changing the Odds Against Women," from *Redbook Magazine*, January 1974, p. 125.

PAYING THE PRICE

It sometimes takes a great deal of thought, preparation, and work to gain success and satisfaction in reaching your goals. In approaching figure control, you must establish a plan for reaching your goals, and it must be a lifelong plan. Your plan will be only as effective as the strength of your commitment to follow it. A commitment requires an investment of time and energy and a willingness to make personal sacrifices.

When you have arrived at the point of converting thought into action, the task ahead will not be easy—that is a fact you must accept in the beginning if you are to experience success in figure control. You will probably have to change several personal habits and preferences.

Far too often we forego judgment, knowledge, and past experience in attempting to control our figures. We allow personal opinions and impulses to control our behavior. Learning to accept change and acknowledging the relationship between cause and effect are possibly the most important steps to a successful experience in figure control.

Your motivation must be strong enough to allow for making changes in your life-style. You should make every effort to identify the interests, needs, and problems from which your motives are derived so that you can establish the practice of reinforcing them at regular intervals. You must also make certain that this is something you *want* to do, for otherwise you will fail.

The woman who is successful in maintaining her figure throughout her lifetime makes a serious commitment to the project. She consistently attempts to replace bad habits with good ones. She is creative in adjusting her habits to meet her needs and interests. She sets realistic goals with respect for her limitations. Her goals are not extreme and she does not undertake to solve all problems at once. Each intermediate goal in the long-range picture is a small victory reinforcing her motivation and level of confidence.

It would be wrong to tell you that you will never experience failure or setbacks. You must learn to accept a measure of failure, for you will fail many times before experiencing the sought-for results. When you fall, learn to pick yourself up, brush yourself off, and get back on the road again. Look up, not down. Try to handle your disappointments and failures with tolerance. Recognize, define, and solve problems, and attempt to follow through with new ideas and new approaches. Control your impulses with knowledge and reasoning. Learn to delay immediate satisfactions as you look toward the success you will experience in accomplishing the goals you have established.

Life is full of choices and decisions. We can choose to "let nature take its course," or we can choose to control our lives by accepting the responsibility for our decisions. The freedom to make wise choices comes from discipline. We believe that self-discipline is one key to success in any endeavor; we know absolutely that this is true in the realm of figure control. To maintain a good figure, a healthy mind, and a strong body you must be prepared to pay the price—in time, hard work, and determination.

Finally, we cannot say enough about the importance of keeping a positive outlook. Strive for enthusiasm in every task you undertake. Far too many of us allow negative ideas to frustrate our most constructive goals. The burden of discovering your happiness rests with you. Keep your thought processes constantly alert, appreciate your own efforts and your strengths, accept the reality of change and know when and how you must adjust to it—and always bear in mind that it's your future you're building.

THE PATHS OF REALITY

Two roads diverged in a wood, and I—
I took the one less traveled by,
And that has made all the difference.

— Robert Frost

The desire for an attractive figure is a very real thing to each one of us. The media barrage of products, services, and books related to weight control and figure contouring is convincing evidence of this fact. As consumers, we are willing to buy all kinds of gimmicks and gadgets guaranteed to help us in our quest. Consequently we look for an easy way to solve our problems, choosing to believe there is a quick and simple solution.

If we happen to have a figure problem, chances are we have also been seduced by at least one of the effortless methods offered to today's affluent consumer who spends or sends her money with the hopeful attitude, "I'll try anything once!" What we are actually buying is the idea that there is a magic formula for achieving the ideal figure. More effort goes in to making believers out of us than in helping us achieve the figure we desire.

7

The promise of losing inches in only one visit to a figure salon or health spa can be very effective in attracting paying customers. How satisfying it is to see astounding results in measurements after your very first visit! But think about it: a tape measure can be very easily manipulated. It can be placed higher or lower on the body or held loosely or tightly, and the person measuring you can easily place one or two fingers under the tape while pulling it together behind your back. Notice that when the measurement is taken at the conclusion of the visit, you are reminded to stand very tall and hold yourself erect so you can be measured at your best. Try this trick yourself and you will see that the inches melt away before your eyes! This is because posture improvement alone will show improvement in measurements taken at the bustline, waist, and hips.

But if we can be impressed with the idea that taking off those extra inches isn't going to be as hard as we imagined, we may consider taking out a membership with the salon. If so, here's another caution: look before you sign that contract. Is it for one year, two years, or even three? There is no way to get out of paying for an unused portion of time. And notice that these types of salons do not guarantee *weight loss*, for a very good reason: it would be impossible to manipulate the scale, which we can read ourselves.

Studios that provide wrapping treatments guarantee loss of inches. Their method is a simple one indeed, based on the displacement of fluid in the body and the loss of fluid from the body. Immediately after the unwrapping, measurements show a loss of inches. This is another trick that you can try at home. You will "lose inches," but this is not permanent loss of fatty tissue; it is merely fluid loss, and as soon as you resume normal activity and consume liquids, you will return to your original measurements. The water-loss myth is one of the most widespread fallacies about weight control. It is *never* more than temporary weight loss, however, regardless of the device used to produce it. Most commonly found among these devices are diuretic pills, sweat and sauna suits, wrapping, and steam baths.

Some salons provide equipment that "does the work for you." Also, you can purchase equipment for home use which advertisements claim can tone your muscles while you relax. Two of these machines should be labeled hazardous: the vibrator-belt and the roller machine, which can damage the skin and tissues by bruising and causing stretch-marks. These machines also have very little real effect and are a waste of time and money.

Among the most ridiculous gimmicks sold to women are the bust-developers, "guaranteed" to increase breast size. The breast is made up of glandular and fatty tissue and the two things affecting its size are heredity and weight. There are no muscles which can be exercised and developed within the breast; thus there is no way to change its size other than through surgery. The muscles lying under the breast, forming the chest wall, can be exercised. The result will strengthen support and minimize bra bulges.

Consumer fascination with exercise gimmicks and body shapers is surpassed only by the incredible number of methods for weight control. There are doctors, drugs, foods, clubs, menus, recipes, and magazines entirely devoted to diet and weight control. Countless fad diets sweep through the country regularly, emphasizing the fact that more than half the American population is said to be concerned with excess weight. This is a concern that large manufacturers and unscrupulous professionals alike have capitalized on.

People seldom take the time to check further than the brand name if the word "diet" is attached to the label. We want to believe that certain foods contain no calories because they are labeled as such. Good examples are the "diet breads" on the market. White enriched diet bread contains an average of seven calories per ounce as compared to regular white enriched bread at eight calories per ounce—only a one-calorie difference. A slice of diet bread is lower in calories simply because of thin slicing. A similar technique is used with recipes and menus. The "diet-label" is attached when the calorie content is only slightly adjusted to provide less calories. To make matters worse, we tend to justify larger or additional servings of food just because we are told they are lower in calories. Learning to check labels for contents is a big step in consumer education.

The group motivation of "diet clubs" provides the necessary incentive for some people to lose weight. However, it can be expensive, time-consuming, and next to impossible for the working woman. A comment commonly heard from people using this method is, "I spend most of the day either shopping or cooking." If the diet organization subscribes to the concept that exercise is detrimental to your diet, you may assume that it intends to keep you around longer, meanwhile charging you periodic membership dues. Diet organizations, however, can be beneficial to the person wanting to learn good nutritional concepts and establish better eating habits. Use good judgment when selecting a diet organization or club.

In addition, women are turning in increasing numbers to "diet clinics" where doctors under the cloak of professional respectability are prescribing all kinds of pills and injections. Some pills actually do curb the appetite for a period of time, but many are habit-forming and dangerous in the long run. At any rate, paying for pills or injections is certainly not a wise lifetime plan for controlling weight.

We must keep in mind that weight control and figure control are not short-term tasks. Lifetime goals must be established. What happens when the diet ends or we stop taking the pills? The greatest feeling of security and satisfaction comes from knowing that we have the power, the determination and self-discipline, to accomplish by ourselves the goals that we set for ourselves.

FOOD-THE FOE

There are loads of magic and miracle diets floating around. A new one periodically makes the rounds, and once again every fat man has a new, easy shortcut cure to try out.

— Theodore Isaac Rubin, M.D.

"Tomorrow I'm going on a diet!" Have you said this to yourself lately? If so, you are not alone, for dieting has become an unwanted hobby for millions of Americans. Our country is probably the most prosperous nation in the world and yet the unhealthiest weight-wise. Food is becoming an enemy in our lives, and when it is combined with our sedentary way of life, it becomes an even greater hazard. Obesity is one of America's major health problems.[1]

---

[1] Theodore Berland, *Rating the Diets* (Skokie, Ill.: Consumer Guide, vol. 53 April 1974), p. 12.

WHAT IS OBESITY?

There are many definitions of obesity. A common one is that the overweight person weighs 10 to 20 percent above the average according to sex, age, and height standards, while the obese person weighs more than 20 percent above the average.[2] Dr. Theodore Isaac Rubin defines obesity as "the psychological condition that leads to overeating and overweight (10 percent or more than the normally accepted weight for your size) for a period of at least ten years."[3] Jean Mayer and Neil Solomon agree that overweight is weight in excess of the normal range, whereas obesity is a condition marked by an excessive accumulation of body fat.[4] Although experts seem to differentiate between overweight and obesity, they unanimously agree that excess fat is hazardous to health and that overeating usually leads to obesity. Therefore, when making reference to any degree of excess fat, we shall use the term obese.

How to Determine Degree of Obesity

There are a number of ways to determine the degree of obesity of an individual. They range from the very technical x-ray and underwater weighing performed in a laboratory, and the use of skinfold calipers, to the more informal Pinch Test. The Pinch Test can be performed on any fatty area of the body, the most common area being the triceps area (back side) of the upper arm. With the arm bent slightly, pinch the skin halfway between the shoulder and the elbow on the underside of the arm, drawing it away from the bone.[5] "When you pinch it you get a double fold, so the thickness should be between half an inch and an inch. If it measures greater than an inch, you're fat."[6] You might try the Pinch Test on other areas too, such as the abdomen, shoulder blade, or back of the calf. However, due to structural differences and inaccuracy in measuring, the Pinch Test is often not reliable. Therefore, we recommend another effective way of determining your degree of fat: look at your image as you stand nude in front of a full-length mirror and just let it all hang loose. The mirror nearly always tells the truth! In addition, we highly recommend that you weigh each morning just after getting out of bed and "going to the bathroom." All scales do not weigh the same, so when comparing weight, always use the same set of scales.

---

[2] Phyllis Howe, *Basic Nutrition in Health and Disease* (Philadelphia: W. B. Saunders, 1971), p. 162.

[3] Theodore Isaac Rubin, *Forever Thin* (New York: Gramercy, 1970) p. 4.

[4] Jean Mayer, *Overweight: Causes, Cost, and Control* (Englewood Cliffs, N.J.: Prentice-Hall, 1968) p. 12; Neil Solomon, *The Truth About Weight Control* (New York: Stein and Day, 1971) p. 19.

[5] Ronald M. Deutsch, *The Family Guide to Better Food and Better Health*, (Des Moines: Meredith Corporation, 1971) p. 102.

[6] Berland, *Rating the Diets*, p. 23.

What Causes Obesity?

There are a number of causes of obesity. "Food is the fuel that keeps the body working. But there is a limit to the amount of fuel the body can use up. When more food is consumed than the body can utilize, the excess is stored as fat."[7] However, we need to look beyond a simple balancing of food intake and energy expenditure for a full explanation of the problem. Only a small percentage of cases are caused by metabolic disfunctioning. Other important causes for obesity include heredity, environment, emotional disturbances, self-indulgence, sedentary living, misinformation, and ignorance of proper eating habits and nutrition. Another possible cause might be damage to the appetite control center in the brain known as the hypothalamus, which may produce overeating and resultant obesity.[8] Whether the cause be organic, psychogenic, or cultural, the factor responsible for obesity is overeating. "The mechanism of regulation of food intake is . . . an extremely complicated one . . . a great many unrelated factors may lead to overeating with resulting obesities."[9] Thus we see that overeating can result from psychological conditions, physiological factors causing the body to burn less calories, or inadequate physical activity. Whatever the reason, it is still overeating.

And whatever the cause of obesity in an individual, the results are discouraging and frustrating. Physically, the body is burdened with additional weight to support and carry. This causes the obese individual to tire easily and to feel uncomfortable and lethargic. Exercise not only requires more effort than it should, but its results are much less apparent to the obese woman, for her figure lies hidden beneath fat. To be sure, the exercise is working, but if its effect is not evident she may give up and, out of discouragement or impatience, either resign herself to her "fate" or join the thousands of other Americans who support that one-hundred-million-dollar market which promotes reducing programs, aids, gadgets, and diets that prey on the ignorance of the obese.

FOOD FADS AND DIET FADS

Who wouldn't be tempted to seek the effortless, dramatic effects promised by a revolutionary diet plan? Food faddism has been defined as "the ascribing to particular foods or diets of powers beyond those they actually have."[10] Fad

---

[7] Barry Ott, "What Do You Think You Are?" in *Fitness for Living* (Emmaus, Penn.: Rodale Press, vol. 4, no. 6, 1970), p. 37.

[8] Ladelle Crawford, "Obesity and Weight Control," in *Introduction to Nutrition* (Berkeley: Fybate Lecture Notes, 1972), p. 36.

[9] Mayer, *Overweight*, p. 58.

[10] Molly Kretsch, "Food Faddism," in *Introduction to Nutrition* (Berkeley: Fybate Lecture Notes, 1972), p. 75.

diets characteristically promise spectacular results and are limited to a particular food or specific food group. The problem with fad diets is generally two-fold: they seldom help to establish eating habits necessary for lifelong weight control, and they are nutritionally inadequate. When essential foods and nutrients are supplied irregularly or are left out entirely for a period of time, the body's metabolism may be changed or upset resulting in the body's inefficiency to use certain foods. This might cause the individual to gain even more weight once off the diet.

For the person susceptible to a particular nutritional imbalance, the wrong kind of diet may have drastic results. The effect of a high-protein diet on a person with a kidney infection or malfunction could be kidney failure or even death. Drinking the enormous quantities of water recommended by certain diets could be dangerous to some people.

In addition to the irrational and unsound nutritional basis of most fad diets, we cannot recommend them because of their constant threat to health. As nutritionist Phyllis Howe has quipped, "the best that can be said for fad diets is that people seldom remain on them long enough to induce malnutrition."[11]

Currently several popular fad diets are passing through the ranks of the obese. Some of these are based on restricting the amount of carbohydrates in the diet. A low carbohydrate diet that does not eliminate carbohydrates entirely can be a good one to follow, and many persons have experienced success with this type of diet. Keep in mind, however, that the calorie intake is affected and, in most cases, is lowered when the carbohydrate intake is less. Whether you count carbohydrate grams or calories, the end result is much the same. You must know your intake of calories in order to control your weight with lasting success.

High carbohydrate diets can have serious ramifications. The most familiar of these are the vegetarian diets and the well-known macrobiotic diet—which, incidentally, has been the cause of several deaths. These diets are high in bulk, but do not necessarily supply an excess of calories or needed nutrients. Foods include natural cereal grains, seeds, nuts, legumes, and several varieties of fruits and vegetables. The final stage of the macrobiotic diet consists totally of cereal grains, preferably rice.

Since vegetarianism is a relatively recent fad in America, we are just now beginning to see the adverse results of some of the more specialized of these diets. These results include, in addition to general loss of energy, such dietary deficiency diseases as anemia, scurvy, pellegra, and rickets.[12] Important vitamins and minerals—including iron, niacin, and frequently vitamin A—may not be

---

[11] Howe, *Basic Nutrition*, p. 162.

[12] Darla Erhard, "The New Vegetarians," in *Nutrition Today* (Annapolis) vol. 8, no. 6, 1973, pp. 11-16.

supplied in the vegetarian diet. Moreover, protein may not be present in adequate form to supply all of the amino acids.[13] Strict vegetarians must attempt to balance their diets with dairy products and eat the proper amounts of the necessary foods. "A diet that avoids animal flesh but that does include milk and eggs poses no serious nutritional problems. One simply changes the source from which protein is derived by adding more cheese, eggs, milk, dry beans, peas, and nuts. . . . Nutritional planning becomes virtually impossible if all animal products are eliminated from the diet. . . . Such a diet has no vitamin B-12 and a limited spectrum of calcium sources."[14] The most appalling result is the recent discovery of numerous cases of malnutrition among the children and babies of strict vegetarians. Nutritionist Darla Erhard has described with words and pictures the sad story of malnourishment that has occurred among these young ones: "the malnourishment is not unlike that seen in developing countries where ignorant mothers follow similar infant feeding practices."[15]

Many persons have successfully lost pounds on the Weight Watchers' program. The diet recommended by this organization is nutritionally sound, but has one drawback—it is time-consuming to stick rigidly to the weighing and measuring which is an important part of Weight Watchers' food preparation. It is difficult for most working people to devote the time needed, and as a result this is a major cause for dropouts. However, it is a good way to begin the discipline and establish the cooking habits that are necessary for lifetime food control.

There are fad diets too numerous to list, such as the Mayo Clinic Diet (not originated by the famed Mayo Clinic), the grapefruit diet (grapefruit has no magic power or special effect on fat), the alcohol diet, the water diet, the eggs and cottage cheese diet, the no-carbohydrate high-fat diets (very high in cholesterol), and many more, we are certain, by the time this book is published. With so many diets rampant in America today it is no wonder that George McGovern, Chairman of the Senate Committee on Nutrition and Human Needs, could say that "Americans are eating less and less well nutritionally."

SOME NUTRITIONAL CONCEPTS

We tend to overlook the fact that nutrition is a science based on the food requirements of the body. Even though the human body will operate and survive on any number of foods, scientific knowledge tells us that there is a specific combination of foods which allows our bodies to operate most efficiently. The

---

[13] Jean Bogert, George Briggs, and Doris Calloway, *Nutrition and Physical Fitness* (Philadelphia: W. B. Saunders, 1973), pp. 431-32.

[14] Erhard, "The New Vegetarians," p. 12.

[15] *Los Angeles Times,* February 18, 1974, Part I, p. 2.

1. *Milk or Milk Products* (2 or more servings). One cup of milk or yogurt, or one and a half cups of cottage cheese, or two or three scoops of ice cream, or a serving of hard cheese (such as Cheddar) equal to about a one-inch cube.

2. *High-Protein Foods* (2 or more servings). A serving is a three-ounce portion of any meat, fish, or poultry, or two eggs. These foods can be alternated with a cup of dry peas or dry beans or lentils, with four tablespoons of peanut butter, or with the 60-odd nuts used to make the peanut butter. Cheese may also be used here if it is not used in the Milk group.

3. *Green or Yellow Vegetables* (2 servings). A half cup is a typical serving. Dark-green or deep yellow vegetables are the best sources of the several nutrients supplied by these foods.

4. *Citrus Fruits, Tomatoes, and Other Good Sources of Vitamin C* (1 serving). A serving is six ounces of citrus juice, with more of tomato juice preferred, an orange or a half a grapefruit, two generous cups of frozen lemonade, or a medium tomato. Two-thirds of a cup of strawberries can be a replacement, a sixth of a medium watermelon, or half a papaya. Or, if you have extra servings from some foods in the Vegetable group, they can be applied here, in one-cup amounts: raw cabbage, collards, kale, kohlrabi, mustard greens, spinach, and turnip greens.

5. *Potatoes and Other Vegetables and Fruits* (1 serving). A serving is a medium potato, an ear of corn, an apple, or a banana; it is usually about a half a cup of such items as cooked, canned, or raw carrots, peaches, pineapple, apricots, beets, lima beans, cauliflower, or a small salad portion of lettuce.

6. *Bread, Flour, and Cereals* (3-4 servings). One serving is a slice of bread, an ounce of ready-to-eat breakfast cereal, one-half to three-fourths of a cup of cooked breakfast cereal, cornmeal, grits, macaroni, noodles, rice, spaghetti, a two-inch biscuit, three-inch cookie, slice of cake, or muffin. (All baked goods should be made with enriched or whole-grain flour; otherwise they may not do their job in this group.) A doughnut, a four-inch pancake, or half a waffle will also serve.

7. *Butter or Margarine* (2-3 servings). A serving is a tablespoon.

8. *Fluids* (3-5 servings). A serving is one cup and includes primarily water-based drinks, such as water, milk, fruit juice, beer, coffee, tea, powdered mixes, carbonated soft drinks.

9. *Sugar Foods* (none needed). One serving is interpreted as three teaspoons of added sugar (as to coffee, fruit), a half-ounce of hard candy, marshmallow, or caramel, and slightly more chocolate. One tablespoon of honey, molasses, two one-inch mints, a tablespoon of syrup (chocolate, maple, corn, etc.), jam or jelly.

well-balanced diet is a scientific fact. It meets the body's requirements. With very few exceptions, these nutritional needs can be met by choosing foods from the food groups on page 15 on a daily basis.[16]

Foods from these groups supply the proper nutrients, or chemical compounds, which your body must have, first for energy and then for growth, maintenance, and repair. It is the total combination of nutrients which is essential to body functions, although each nutrient has its specific function. Even though foods supply more than one type of nutrient, they are generally classified according to their most prominent nutrient. If you are trying to lose weight, be sure to choose from among the lowest-calorie foods.

The following discussion is an attempt to identify the terms and some of the principles that are most important to weight control and basic nutrition. We encourage you to complete your technical knowledge in nutrition from the books listed at the end of this chapter. The major classes of nutrients are as follows (remember, the quality of your foods is reflected by the nutrients they contain):

Carbohydrates are the major source of energy and are easily digested, unlike fats. If the body takes in more carbohydrates than it needs to meet its immediate energy requirement, they are stored as fat. Carbohydrates are the sugars, starches, fruits, and vegetable bulk provided in our diets. Cereal grains and breads contribute a large part of our carbohydrate intake, as do milk and milk products.

Proteins provide the amino acids that are essential to the building and growth of new tissues; they are needed for tissue maintenance and repair, for the production of enzymes and some hormones, for the production of milk, and for energy. Animal proteins, including milk, meat, fish, poultry, and eggs, are complete proteins containing all essential amino acids that must be provided through the diet. Animal proteins are frequently high in fats as well. Nuts, cereal grains, and legumes provide incomplete protein, meaning that they do not contain all of the essential amino acids. Excess protein can be used for energy and will be stored as fat.

Fats are a significant source of energy. Although fat content increases calories, a diet must include some fat in order to provide the essential fatty acid linoleic, which cannot be synthesized in the body and is needed for growth and skin. Fats also carry the fat-soluble vitamins: (A, D, E, and K), and enhance the flavor of many foods by providing a more lasting feeling of fullness since they remain in the digestive tract longer. Foods containing visible fat are butter, oil, and meat. Invisible fats are found in chocolate, nuts, egg yolk, dairy products, and bakery goods. We must be aware that animal fats contain significant

---

[16] Deutsch, *Family Guide to Better Food*, p. 8.

amounts of cholesterol, which appears to be related to heart disease. Because cholesterol is normally manufactured by the body in the quantity it needs, a limited fat content in the diet is important.

Vitamins assist in the regulation of the chemical processes of the body. They are required in very small quantities, but they must be replaced frequently since the body does not manufacture them. The two major groups of vitamins are the fat-soluble vitamins (A, D, E, and K), which are easily stored in the body, and the water-soluble vitamins (B-complex and C), which are not stored but instead are eliminated readily from the body. Vitamins aid in normal reproduction, promote growth, aid in tissue repair, help prevent infection, and help maintain the general health of the body. Vitamins are present in many foods, but the best sources are fresh fruits and vegetables, cereals, and grains. They are also supplied by ultra-violet light (D), carotene (A), and the bacteria of the intestines (K). Food storage and preparation are important in retaining the naturally occurring nutrients in foods. Over-cooked, over-processed, and refined foods are often almost depleted of both vitamins and minerals. For this reason, it is suggested that a good multiple vitamin be taken on the average of two or three times a week if the majority of the diet consists of processed foods. However, the excessive use of vitamins or the taking of large doses of a particular vitamin is not recommended, since research has not yet shown this to be effective. The Federal Food and Drug Administration has issued Recommended Daily Allowances (RDA) of medically determined vitamin and mineral needs, and this list is a useful guide in planning your menus.

Minerals play a role much like vitamins. They are important to the growth and maintenance of the body's structures—bones, teeth, muscles, brain cells, dermal tissues, blood cells, and nerve cells. A diet based on the food groups list above will generally provide an adequate supply of minerals. The minerals found to be most frequently lacking in the diet are iron, calcium, and fluorine. The need for iron is highest among infants and women. During pregnancy it is important that a woman have adequate supplies of iron to supply both herself and the unborn child. Iron deficiency is a common problem among women and adolescent girls, and the diet may have to be supplemented from time to time with foods of high iron concentration.

Calories are simply measures of energy (heat energy). When the body moves, energy is used, with the source of that energy being food. In order to maintain weight, the number of calories used must balance the number of calories consumed by eating. You will gain weight if you consume more calories in food than you use up during activity. You will lose weight if the reverse is true. There is nothing magic about the calorie, but no reason to fear it, either. Neither will calories disappear simply because you refuse to recognize that they exist. Remember, they are merely a measurement tool.

THE METABOLIC FACTOR

Metabolism is another term often used in connection with weight control. Frankly, we hear it used far too often as an excuse for weight problems. The few cases of obesity that are caused by metabolic disorders should be treated by a physician. Metabolism is a complex process, not a simple excuse. The conversion of fuel to energy and the body's process of using that energy is called metabolism; the basic metabolic rate (BMR) is the amount of energy consumed while the body is in a resting state. Remember that changing fuel into energy is nothing more than using calories. Keeping this information in mind, let's discuss some of the facts about weight control.[17]

1.   Women have a lower basic metabolic rate than men and children by about 10 percent. This creates a problem, since most women cook for families whose metabolic rate is higher than their own. These women will have to eat less than their men and their children do, and this can be difficult. It *can* be done, though, and it becomes less of a problem for the woman who is aware of this fact.

2.   When we are sleeping, our metabolic rate drops by about 10 percent. This means that we should consume our calories during our active hours and perhaps make the evening meal our light one. A good rule-of-thumb is to refrain from eating during the four hours before bedtime.

3.   As we age, our basic metabolic rate declines gradually. In order to control our weight as we age, we must consume fewer calories or increase our level of activity. How many times have you heard, "slow down as you get older?" Do that and you'll be fat!

4.   A rise in body temperature causes a rise in metabolic rate. Exercise causes an increase in the metabolic rate which, in turn, causes the body's temperature to increase. Therefore, more exercise each day will mean that you will be able to consume more calories without gaining weight, or it will aid in your usage of calories if you are trying to lose weight. When weight loss is your objective, exercise will speed the result.

5.   The thyroid gland regulates the rate of metabolism, and changes in thyroid activity are reflected in the metabolic rate. The condition of the thyroid should be checked only by a competent physician who has accurate methods for measuring thyroid activity. It can be very dangerous to take thyroid pills when you don't need them.

6.   Undernourished persons are likely to have a lowered basic metabolic rate. Therefore, avoid starvation diets and fasting! In proportion, the number of calories used during these states is lower anyway, so why jeopardize your health?

---

[17] Corrine H. Robinson, *Normal and Therapeutic Nutrition* (New York: Macmillan, 1972), p. 95.

7.   The basic metabolic range for normal adults is about 1300 to 1700 calories a day, with the woman's range falling closer to the 1300 level. This should give you an idea of how many calories you can consume each day without gaining weight. Use this fact as a starting point and go from there. Refer to the energy expenditure guide included in the Appendix to this book and add to the basic metabolic rate the cost of your activities for a day. This will give you an idea of how many calories you can consume.

THE PATH TO FOLLOW

The science of nutrition, which is the fundamental knowledge that our bodies require certain foods to be nourished and to operate, must be the basis for our eating habits. The phrase "well-balanced diet" refers to a pattern of eating habits which, once established, will see us through a lifetime. To help you build those habits, here are our suggestions. It will take time, planning, patience, and effort *every day of your life* to maintain eating habits that will control your weight.

First, and perhaps most important from your standpoint, is the hard, cold fact that you are going to have to make some changes. You will have to give in a little and give up a little, sometimes a lot! Keep the rewards in mind constantly and assure yourself that you *can* change. A lot of us have! Instead of continuing to fear change, do it and then you won't have to fear it any longer!

You must follow a food control plan that is sensible instead of sensational —a food control plan for life. As we see it, this plan must be more than simply nutritious; it must also be adaptable to suit different tastes, individual needs, and special problems. We cannot give you a specific diet or menu to follow, for your diet and menus must really be your own or you won't be able to follow them forever. We have given you a list of books, some of which contain a sample diet or sample menus, and we will give you several suggestions and hints about how to go about setting up an eating plan.

Begin designing your individual plan with the calorie and be sure to include the foods you are used to eating, modifying them according to calorie count, but not eliminating them completely. For instance, you can make a lower-calorie spaghetti sauce. Try lean beef browned in its own fat instead of in oil or butter; add onions, stewed tomatoes (no tomato sauce or paste), canned mushrooms with the liquid included, some water, and your own choice of seasonings. Cook as usual, and you have a relatively lower-calorie spaghetti sauce.

In the beginning, you must keep a diary of the calories you consume each day. There are several reasons for this record-keeping. First, you will see exactly how many calories you are eating; you will avoid the temptation of guessing. Next, you will learn the caloric content of foods, so that you can make wise food choices. As you read over your diary or record, you will recognize the areas where calories can be cut and suitable eating patterns will begin to emerge. Your record will show which of the food groups is supplying the bulk of your diet and whether your diet is balanced. This is information that you must have at hand in order to reshape your future eating habits. Remember, in most cases, reshaping your eating habits is the first step toward reshaping your figure. There will come a time when you will not have to make entries in your diary every day, but whenever problems reappear, start using your diary regularly again!

One pound of fat equals 3500 calories. This fact tells you that you must use 3500 more calories than you eat in order to lose a pound of fat. We recommend a gradual weight loss of one pound per week. This seemingly moderate goal is medically sound and would require a genuine modification of eating and activity habits. This can be accomplished by eliminating 500 calories per day from your food intake, or by eliminating 250 calories per day of food and using 250 more calories a day through added activities (see the energy expenditure guide). How much is 500 calories in food? Two waffles equal 450 calories, while four doughnuts are 475. Two cups of cocoa are over 500 calories. One piece of strawberry cream pie is worth 950 calories. Does that give you an idea? Beware of so-called dietetic, non-fat, or low-calorie foods. For instance, some non-fat yogurts contain more calories than low-fat yogurts. Dietetic cookies are seldom much lower in calories than the same type of regular cookies. Because dietetic foods are often very expensive, and because in some cases the labels are misleading, we suggest that you stick to regular foods that are low in calories, checking your calorie guide to make sure.

To calculate your caloric need, we would remind you again that you must determine the amount of energy (calories) you spend in activity each day. In your calorie-intake diary you should also keep a record of your own activity expenditure, using the calories-per-hour figures given in our energy expenditure guide. It will not be exact, but it will be a close average. Add up the calories spent in normal activity and any additional physical activity; include everything from sleeping to watching TV. Then compare your caloric expenditure with your caloric intake, and this will tell you how far away you are from that all-important balance. This tally should be kept over a period of several days in order to determine a representative average.

If by comparison your tally shows a lower calorie intake than calorie expenditure, you should be on the way to shedding a few pounds. However, if you do not lose weight, we suggest that you recheck your food intake by measuring food amounts with extreme accuracy. You will also want to recheck your activity schedule. This is what is meant when we say that *planning a diet requires time and effort!*

Now some final suggestions. Eliminate all eating between meals and reduce the tasting of foods that you are preparing. (It's a good idea to have someone do the tasting for you.) If you consume more calories in one day than you should, consume less during the next day; this will balance the excess. Always leave something on your plate and keep the portions small. Get up from the table immediately after you finish eating—it's just too easy to nibble if you stay. Keep the right kinds of foods in the house and by all means *don't be afraid to say NO!* And when you are tempted to sit down with popcorn and potato chips for an evening of television, remember these words of Dr. Jean Mayer: "Every farmer worth his salt knows that the best way to fatten an animal is to feed it and keep it penned up. The less activity, the more weight you get from eating the same amount of food. I'm afraid that this is just what our society is doing to far too many of our people."[18]

Recommended References

The following books contain complete information on nutrition and weight control, including food-value and calorie guides and energy expenditure tables.

Bogert, L. Jean, Briggs, George M., and Calloway, Doris H. *Nutrition and Physical Fitness.* Philadelphia: W. B. Saunders, 1973.

Deutsch, Ronald M. *The Family Guide to Better Food and Better Health.* Des Moines: Meredith Corporation (Better Homes and Gardens Creative Home Library), 1971.

Howe, Phyllis S. *Basic Nutrition in Health and Disease.* Philadelphia: W. B. Saunders, 1971.

Martin, Ethel Austin. *Nutrition in Action.* San Francisco: Holt, Rinehart and Winston, 1971.

Mayer, Jean. *Overweight: Causes, Cost, and Control.* Englewood Cliffs, N.J.: Prentice-Hall, 1968.

Robinson, Corrine H. *Normal and Therapeutic Nutrition.* New York: Macmillan, 1972.

Williams, Sue Rodwell. *Nutrition and Diet Therapy.* Saint Louis: C. V. Mosby, 1969.

The following book contains complete information concerning the popular fad diets. It also includes the above information.

Berland, Theodore. *Rating the Diets.* Skokie, Ill.: Consumer Guide, vol. 53, April 1974.

The following books are calorie and carbohydrate references only.

Kaufman, William I. *Brand-Name Guide to Calories and Carbohydrates.* New York: Pyramid Books, 1973.

Kraus, Barbara. *The Dictionary of Calories and Carbohydrates.* New York: Grosset and Dunlap, 1973.

Wexler, Joan. *No-Guess Calorie Counter.* New York: Bantam Books, 1969. (This is a pocket guide.)

---

[18] Jean Mayer, "Inactivity—Key to Overweight Youth," in *Los Angeles Times,* February 21, 1974.

The following books are excellent references for diet and menu planning. They contain recipes as well as calorie guides.

Better Homes and Gardens Calorie Counter's Cookbook. Des Moines: Meredith Corporation, 1970.

Better Homes and Gardens Eat and Stay Slim. Des Moines: Meredith Corporation, 1972.

Gibbons, Barbara. *Creative Low-Calorie Cooking.* New York: Family Circle, Inc., 1973.

Schoenberg, Hazel P. *Cookbook for Calorie Watchers.* New York: Good Housekeeping Books, 1971.

The following are excellent references concerning the psychology of weight control.

Bruno, Frank F. *Think Yourself Thin.* New York: Harper and Row Publishers, 1972.

Rubin, Theodore Isaac. *Forever Thin.* New York: Gramercy, 1970.

Solomon, Neil. *The Truth About Weight Control.* New York: Stein and Day, 1971.

Stuart, Richard B. and Davis, Barbara. *Slim Chance in a Fat World: Behavioral Control of Obesity.* Champaign, Ill.: Research Press, 1972.

Wyden, Peter and Wyden, Barbara. *How the Doctors Diet.* New York: Pocket Books, 1972.

POSTURE – SLUMP NOW, PAY LATER

It isn't what I do, but how I do it.
It isn't what I say, but how I say it.
And how I look when I do and say it.

— Mae West

Whether your exercise is for figure or for fitness, you should always exercise the habit of good posture. Posture is the structural basis for your figure and contributes to the proper functioning of several physiological processes within your body. Along with its importance physically, posture reflects your physical personality and how you feel about yourself.

You may already have a general idea of what posture is all about, and may be tempted to dismiss the subject in favor of a more challenging one. We hope you will not, because an explanation of the far-reaching effects posture has on your body is truly impressive.

WHAT IS POSTURE?

Posture is a general term referring to the way in which the weight of the body is

23

distributed through its center of gravity. "Good posture" involves aligning the body from head to toe: the distribution of weight must be balanced from front to back and from side to side in order for the body to be in proper alignment. The placement or "alignment" of various parts of the body is critical in maintaining postural balance. Here is the ideal alignment, from the ground up:

1.   Feet: Parallel with toes straight ahead. The ankle and foot should meet squarely at right angles, indicating even distribution of weight directly through the ankle. (Note: check the soles of your shoes, especially the heels, for signs of uneven wear indicating poor distribution of weight.)

2.   Knees: Neither flexed (bent) nor hyperextended (locked), but loose and held straight.

3.   Seat and abdomen: Hips tucked down and forward, stomach pressed in as when holding a deep breath. This is the basis for straightening curves in the lower back, thus eliminating protruding buttocks and abdomen. Think Thin!

4.   Shoulders and chest: Upright yet relaxed, chest and rib cage lifted but not exaggerated by an arch in the back. Develop a constant awareness of holding the torso erect. Don't give in to slouching when standing or sitting. Think Proud!

5.   Head and neck: Centered squarely above the shoulders, the head balanced evenly with chin parallel to the floor. Avoid tucking the chin or leaning head forward. Think Tall!

When one of these checkpoints is poorly aligned, weight distribution is unevenly directed to your body's base of support. The result is unnecessary strain on muscles, bones, and joints, greater wear and tear on your body—and fatigue.

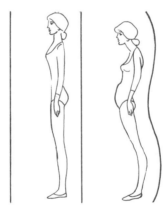

Fig. 4-1

The fashion world is partly responsible for the posture problem shown in Figure 4-1. The typical model's stance has the same casual slump. We see and imitate! This causes the back to sway, creating a lumbar curvature of the spine, or "sway back," and weakening the abdominal muscles. In addition, the shoulders may round forward, pressing in on the chest and rib cage. The ever-present effect of gravity pulling down on your body makes it easy to relax into this slouched position. It is work to stand up straight!

WHY EXERCISE FOR POSTURE?

The structural support for body alignment is provided by your skeletal framework. Muscles do the work of keeping your weight balanced and maintaining structural alignment. Your muscles, however, are creatures of habit. If they are not conditioned to work, they become lazy and weak. Opposing groups of muscles (muscles on the opposite sides of the body or limbs) compensate each other; if one group weakens, the other group grows overly strong and pulls the figure out of alignment. For example, when the abdominal muscles are relaxed, the back muscles tighten, causing a hollow back. To correct the imbalance between two groups of muscles on opposite sides of your body, you must choose strength exercises to bring weak muscles back into shape and flexibility exercises to stretch muscles that are pulling the figure out of alignment. In the example described, the abdominals could be strengthened with sit-ups and the back muscles stretched with the pretzel exercise.

A POSTURE INVENTORY

Good posture is a personal achievement and demands a continuous effort which only *you* can give. The first step in establishing good posture is to take your own posture inventory *in front of a mirror.* From both a front and a side view, check how you *normally* stand and note the position of the posture checkpoints. Now assume the correct posture shown in Figure 4-1 and make a mental note of the adjustments that you must make between your everyday posture and the correct posture.

The next step is to put your thoughts and feelings to work on improvement. This means acquiring a constant awareness of how you are sitting and standing, then constant practice improving your posture and eliminating poor habits. You may be able to correct some bad habits just by becoming aware of them: for instance, uneven weight distribution of the feet, locking the knees, or jutting the chin forward. Other corrections will take more time and specific exercises. Exercises for stretching the muscles are described in Chapter Nine. It will be helpful to use a posture inventory like the one contained in the Appendix (Chart 2). On this chart you can identify your posture problems and keep a record of the exercises in this book that are designed to correct those problems.

POSTURE AND YOUR FIGURE

Good posture is part of making the most of what you have and enhancing the natural proportions of your figure. Figure bulges, bumps, and lumps are often caused by incorrect sitting and standing. Remember, form follows function! If you are overweight, you will call less attention to your size and shape if you carry yourself with the poise of good body alignment. Incorrect posture is never a cover-up for figure problems, and may even accentuate the flaws.

You will be convinced of the relationship between your posture and your figure if you will try this simple experiment. All you need is a tape measure. Allow your abdominal muscles to relax and your pelvis to roll forward. Your shoulders and head will naturally move forward into a slouched position. Measure your bustline, waist, and hips. Now straighten up into good posture: tuck under the hips, pull in the abdominals, lift the rib cage and shoulders. Now measure again and compare the dimensions. This is one of the tricks used by some exercise salons which guarantee a loss of inches in "just one visit." You are distracted from thinking about your posture when they measure you *before* their treatment and reminded to "stand up straight and tall" when measured at the end of the visit.

POSTURE PHYSIOLOGY

Good posture means aligning the skeletal framework to lessen the friction of bone against bone. However, it is not only bones that are involved; shortened muscles may also rub against each other, causing muscular aches and pains.

Back pain, for example, is commonly associated with the muscular imbalance of poor posture. When the muscles extending the length of the spine are strained from constant pulling, you may experience pain in the shoulder and neck as well as in the back. Even headaches can be caused by shortened muscles in the back. Low back pain is frequently caused by shortened muscles in the backs of the legs. The high heels on today's shoes are a major cause of this trouble. The lifted position of the heel constantly puts the calf in a slightly contracted position; when the shoes are removed and the heel is flat on the floor, your calf is actually stretching. Muscle strain may continue up the leg to the lower back.

When the vertebrae in the spinal column are pulled into a curve by overly strong back muscles, an uneven distribution of stress results on the individual vertebra. With time, the uneven wearing of bones caused by stress on the spinal column may cause the pinching of a nerve or even a slipped disc, which could send you to a hospital for corrective surgery. This sort of expense and discomfort can almost always be avoided by working to correct your postural alignment before it becomes a problem.

Next, you should realize that a weakened abdominal wall is partially responsible for most back problems. As postural muscles, the abdominals assist in keeping the back straight, but they have many additional functions of equal importance. They hold the internal organs in place, they support digestive functioning, and they assist the muscles with which breathing is accomplished. These physiological processes, so important to all physical functioning, are less efficient when the abdominal muscles are weak.

As a woman who may someday carry and bear children, you should understand the importance of a straight back and strong abdominal muscles during pregnancy. A straight back enables a woman to carry her baby, both before and after childbirth, with less strain. The environment in which you carry your unborn child is more secure and protected when it is held close in to your body. Delivery will be more natural and safe. And regaining your figure after childbirth will be easier if abdominal muscles are in good shape *before* pregnancy.

The physical personality you project to others comes across in various ways, and the physical presence and poise of good posture is one of them. Poise projects a positive-thinking individual who shows self-confidence. A well-balanced figure reflects the sort of self-respect and pride that are attractive in any situation. Good posture is established by making its practice as habitual as breathing. Don't make excuses for not getting started. The benefits to be enjoyed from the habit of good posture are too close at hand.

EXERCISE –
HOW IT WORKS

*Inactivity is one of the great indignities
of life. Through inactivity people lose
their self-respect, their integrity.*

— Joan Crawford

The secret to figure control is movement—but it must be the right kind of movement. Exercise is movement designed to maintain, change, and improve our bodies. The study of the human body and the ways in which it responds to exercise is a complex branch of science and much too technical to cover in this book. For those who are interested in gaining a more thorough knowledge, a list of books is recommended at the end of this chapter. What we shall do here is answer some basic questions about exercise in order to provide you with a general understanding of the physiology of it.

Why Is Exercise Important?
Your body is a readily adaptable organism. During the natural processes of growth and aging, it is constantly changing, either developing or deteriorating, in

relationship to the physical demands with which it must cope. When no physical demands are made upon your body, its potential and ability to function decline. Chances are that your daily routine does not demand much of you physically. In order to maintain your physical efficiency you must *create* a demand on your system; this can be done through some planned form of physical activity or exercise. Indirectly, exercise is a stimulus for all of the functions of your body. It keeps body processes operating efficiently and smoothly, which is a large part of staying healthy.

Why Is Exercise So Important to Figure Control?

There are two major reasons. First, exercise helps burn the calories that would otherwise be stored as fat, so it can be a significant factor in controlling your weight. Second, and more directly, exercise is responsible for giving you shape because it shapes, tones, and contours your muscles, and muscles are what give shape to your body.

Is All Exercise the Same?

Definitely not! Exercise is specific and there are three basic categories: (1) *Muscular strength and muscular endurance exercises.* These give you your shape because they strengthen and tone your muscles—which is why we call them "figure exercises." These exercises are fully explained in Chapter Seven. (2) *Flexibility exercises.* These stretch and lengthen your muscles and enable you to maintain a full range of movement in the joints as you age—which is why we call this the "youth exercise." Chapter Nine contains a full explanation of flexibility exercise. (3) *Cardiovascular endurance exercise.* This is probably the most important of the three types because it is the only one that really works on the heart muscle—which is why we call it the "life exercise." See Chapter Eight for a full explanation of this kind of exercise.

Is It Important to Do All Three Types of Exercise?

Definitely so! A good figure is not worth much if you are not alive to enjoy it. And by the same token, if you allow yourself to become inflexible as you age, you will not enjoy living nearly as much as you should. You want to create a *whole* individual, not one that is put together in parts.

What Insures Improvement in Exercise?

You will respond specifically to the amount and the kinds of exercise you take part in. The key to improvement is to increase the intensity of the exercise by repeating it a greater number of times, or for a longer period of time, or using a greater workload. There are two terms which explain this. The first is *overload,* which means, very simply, an increase in the intensity of the exercise each time you do it. It applies to each of the three types of exercise. To overload a strength exercise, you repeat it more often or increase the resistance to it. To overload a flexibility exercise, you hold the position longer. To overload an endurance exercise, you keep doing it longer or at a greater speed. The second term is *progression;* it is simply the consistent application of the overload principle. It means having a plan and sticking with it. It means also to continue your exercises if you expect to improve.

What Is Meant by Muscular Contraction and Muscle Tone?
We have said that muscle tone simply means giving shape to the muscles. A contraction is the shortening or tightening of a muscle. You contract your muscles when you do strength exercises, and this is what causes you to develop muscle tone. Muscle tone, or tonus, is the natural tension that exists within your muscle even when it is in a relaxed state.

What Type of Exercise Will Improve the Figure?
Exercises which strengthen your muscles are also those which shape and contour your figure. When muscles contract against a force or resistance, they will be strengthened. You may be pushing or pulling, or lifting an object, a body part, or a weight. If you are moving during the exercise, it is an *isotonic* exercise. If you are not moving but your muscles are contracting, the exercise is *isometric* in nature. Isotonic exercise has the advantage of being longer-lasting; with isometric exercise, results are seen more quickly. Because isometrics can be done in a confined space, they are good to use when you are on the job, or when you need to be inconspicuous. However, you should remember that isometrics burn far fewer calories than exercises which involve bodily movement; and there is no way they can give you a perfect figure in "six minutes a day."

Why Are Muscles Important to the Figure?
Muscles are the underlying tissues in your body which are alternately contracting and relaxing to make you move. As we have said, muscular contraction will contour and tone the muscles. In short, muscles are what give your figure shape; a shapely muscle means a shapely you! The condition or shape of the muscle, not the size, is determined by its use. Muscles that are not used will waste away or *atrophy.* An atrophied muscle appears loose and flabby.

Will Exercise Build Bulky Muscles or Produce a Masculine Appearance?
This is an important question because the fear of becoming larger and "masculine" has kept many women from exercising. Exercise affects only the condition of the muscle, *not* the size. The size of your muscles is determined by factors such as heredity, hormones, weight, and sex. As a woman, you need never worry about building large, bulging muscles because the hormones that govern your

muscular structure are very different from a man's. Structurally, a woman has fewer fibers within each muscle than a man has, which also means that she has less potential for strength development. Each muscle is made up of thousands of these tiny, hair-like fibers, which can support up to a thousand times their own weight! Hence, if compared with a man, a woman of equal size and weight with the same history of physical activity would not be as strong.

The predominantly male hormone testosterone plays a major role in determining the mass and bulkiness of muscles. In women this hormone is present, but in such small amounts that it has virtually no effect on muscle size. Testosterone, like other anabolic steroids, has been produced synthetically and has been taken by some athletes to stimulate development of muscle mass and strength. Another biological difference is that a woman has a thicker layer of fat deposited around her muscles, which gives her a softer appearance and feel. Men's muscles are more sharply defined and firmer. Chemically, the elements within each sex's muscles differ, although the significance of this has not yet been fully explained.

How Do Muscles Work?
Muscles require oxygen, which is supplied by the blood, in order to contract. Contraction requires energy and produces heat which helps to maintain body temperature. This is why you feel warm when you begin to exercise, and why movement keeps you warm when it is cold outside. Muscles work in pairs, one flexing or bending a joint and the other extending or straightening it.

Will Flexibility Exercises Contour the Figure?
Stretching exercises are for flexibility; they won't do much toward shaping your figure. They are important to your mobility, because flexibility keeps your movement free and unrestricted. When it is easy for you to move, you are more likely to keep moving. When your movement is stiff and restricted, you are more likely to curtail your movement.

What Is Meant by the "Stretch Reflex"?
Your muscles will automatically react against being stretched. Tiny receptors are located in the muscles to keep them from over-stretching and to aid in posture control. Sudden stretching stimulates several receptors at once, leading to an exaggerated contraction. This does not occur when the stretch is made gradually. That is why we do not recommend ballistic, or bouncing, stretching movements. Using a repeated bounce to achieve flexibility is not as effective because of the stretch reflex. Also if the stretch reflex should "let go" as you are bouncing, you may overpull and tear muscle fibers. For this reason, ballistic stretch movements are more likely to cause soreness.

What Is a "Static-stretch" Exercise?

Static means non-moving, and stretch means to lengthen or pull. Therefore, static-stretch refers to an exercise involving a stretching movement where you gradually pull into the position and hold without moving for at least a minute.

What Causes Inflexibility?

When your muscles are constantly contracted during normal activity and exercise, the muscles and tendons shorten. If there is a lack of regular movement for a length of time, the range of movement of the joints is inhibited. Muscles become tight and more susceptible to injury, especially tearing and pulling, when joints are inflexible. A good example is one who has just had an elbow cast removed: it will be difficult, if not impossible, to straighten the arm right away if the cast has been on for several weeks.

Why Do Muscles Cramp During Exercise?

They are simply telling you they are lazy and they don't like the exercise. Cramps often occur when you are not used to the activity, and they are nothing to worry about. Just stop long enough to knead the cramped area until the cramp goes away, then continue exercising. If you quit each time you cramp, you will never get past that point in exercise.

Is It Normal to Feel Tired and Sore After Exercise?

Yes, especially in the beginning. It also depends on the amount and type of exercise. The new demands placed on the body cause temporary fatigue, which disappears when the body is able to adjust to the new schedule of exercise. This is the overload principle in operation.

Will Exercise Change Fat into Muscle?

Absolutely not! Fatty tissue and muscular tissue are not the same thing and are not interchangeable. Your chances of converting fat into muscle are about the same as learning to see with your ears.

Is It Normal to Experience a Gain in Weight
When Beginning an Exercise Program?

Yes, but only temporarily. In most cases, the gain is due to fluid retention caused by the soreness of your muscles. Also remember that muscle tissue weighs more than fat but *consumes less space.*

Will Exercise Alone Promote Weight Loss?

No. As stated in Chapter Three, most excess weight will have to be removed through diet. Exercise will redistribute the weight you are already carrying on your body, but it is merely an aid to losing weight. The important thing is your diet and food control.

Is It Possible to Spot Reduce?
No. Evidence shows that spot reducing is a claim, not a fact. Basically, our heredity determines the distribution of fat deposits on our bodies, and also how and when those fat deposits will be used. This is why each of us loses and gains weight differently. We all have our problem areas.

Are There Exercises Which Accomplish More than One Purpose?
Yes. Many endurance activities, for example, will involve the large muscle groups of the body, helping to shape them and your figure, while also working on your cardiovascular system; in addition, they will burn many calories, thus promoting weight loss. A few exercises will combine strength and flexibility. For example, the knee-to-nose sit-up (Chapter Seven, p. 46) will shape the hip, thigh, and abdominals and will also stretch the muscles in the back of the leg. The waist twist (Chapter Seven, p. 50) will contour the torso and provide flexibility in the upper back. These combination exercises are particularly good ones to do because of their double benefits.

Will Strength or Flexibility Exercise Benefit the Heart?
Unfortunately, not much. The heart itself is a specialized type of muscle and it is extremely important that you exercise it properly. Exercise for the cardiovascular system is called endurance exercise, but don't confuse cardiovascular endurance with muscular endurance. Muscular endurance refers to a particular muscle's ability to repeat a movement several times, and it is closely related to a muscle's strength capacity; cardiovascular endurance comes from exercise that strengthens the heart.

Are There Exercises to Relieve Mental or Emotional Tension?
Yes, very specific ones! Tension from the stresses of everyday living can wind up as tension and fatigue within your body. First, you must learn to control this build-up of tension by identifying the cause. Then you can work toward releasing the tension. We must learn to put our conscious processes of relaxation to work on controlling the release of tension. A good outlet for tension is regular recreational activity, re-"creating" a store of strength for mind and emotions. Relaxation will be discussed at length in Chapter Nine.

Is It Possible to Feel Rejuvenated after Exercise?
Very definitely. This feeling of rejuvenation is common, especially after the first few weeks of exercise. The support systems of your body are stimulated by exercise. Your metabolism increases as well. The heart delivers increased

amounts of blood throughout the body and, in exchange, the circulatory system eliminates wastes more quickly. The result is unexpected: you feel like you have more energy instead of less!

What Effects Will Time and Aging Have?

In order to maintain strength and muscle tone, and for weight control, exercise will continue to be a significant factor in your life. Not only does metabolism decrease with age, making it more difficult to maintain your desired weight, but the number of active cells in the body will decrease also. This means the body spends energy supporting inefficient tissue. Weight control becomes increasingly important for the continued health and well-being of your body. The less active we become, the more limited our range of movement is. Flexibility is maintained only through the proper movements. Since injury and healing become more serious with age, the preventive factor of maintaining flexibility becomes more valuable. The deteriorating effects of time are compounded by the normal tendency to become more sedentary. Establishing exercise as a regular habit early in life will help you to maintain your health and body to a greater degree and for a longer time.

What is Important in Planning an Exercise Program?

There is no magic formula for figure control that works for everyone. However, we can offer a few realistic guidelines that can be individually adjusted, and some suggestions that may be useful in establishing goals.

1. *Keep an up-to-date record of your weight.* You should measure weight daily. Weigh at approximately the same time of day, preferably the first thing in the morning. Weigh without any clothes on. A record of your weight will create an awareness of weight increases before they become major problems.

2. *Keep a weekly record of your measurements.* Changes in your weight without concurrent changes in proportion indicate that you are not getting the exercise you need to complement your weight control program. Use the same tape measure each time.

3. *Record your food intake daily and tally calories at the end of each day.* Remember, in order to lose weight you must take in fewer calories than you expend through activity. Determine the average number of calories you are taking in and the major sources for any extra calories over and above your needs.

4. *Determine the amount of calories you use in a normal day.* Use the energy expenditure chart in the Appendix (Chart 1) to keep a record of your total calorie expenditure. In order to maintain your present weight, this expenditure must match each day's calorie intake. In order to lose weight, the calorie expenditure must be greater than the calorie intake.

5. *Determine a regular program of exercise.* To complete your figure program, the rest of your efforts must go into a regular program of exercise. Your

program should include a balance of exercises from each of the chapters on exercise.

6. *Keep a record of your exercises.* A record of the intensity, duration, and repetitions of each exercise will give you a basis for evaluating your progress and the effectiveness of your program. Your current physical condition will determine the starting point for your exercises. Choose exercises which you can do and repeat them until it becomes a real effort to do any more. When you find that it is becoming easier to complete the exercise, you must either make the exercise more strenuous or choose a more difficult exercise. As your body adjusts, improvement will continue only if you progressively increase the exercise load.

7. *Evaluate your exercise program constantly.* In the beginning stages, improvement will occur rapidly. It becomes more difficult to continue the rate of improvement as you progress. Constant evaluation and change will help overcome the plateaus of slow improvement. Once your goals have been met, overload is no longer your guiding principle. Exercises should continue to be done regularly, but on a more diversified basis. To maintain your level of conditioning, it becomes important to maintain your level of interest. Therefore, it is recommended that *regular exercise* supplement various physical activities which are strenuous enough to give your body vigorous activity.

How Often Is Exercise Needed?

This, of course, depends on the type of exercise you are doing and its purpose. If you are working toward improvement, exercise must be done daily. You will begin to lose the effects of your exercise in approximately two days of no exercise. Thus, a minimum program must plan for exercise at least every other day. The key to exercise is that it be done regularly, with a minimum of three times per week.

What Is the Best Time of Day to Exercise?

There is no particular time of day which is best for exercising, but there is one time to avoid, if possible. This is the time directly following your meals. When you are digesting foods, the blood supply to the digestive tract is increased. When vigorous activity is imposed on your system, it also requires increased amounts of blood to be sent to the major muscle groups involved in exercise. Both demands for blood cannot easily be met at the same time, so it is best that you wait for at least one hour after eating before you exercise.

How About a Weight Chart?

Finding a realistic guide for today's ideal slender figure is no easy task. The charts most commonly used are generally based on averages, and the average person in America today is overweight. Therefore, most weight charts are not based on "ideal figures." You will find an "ideal figure" weight chart in the Appendix to this book (Chart 3). Our years of experience with literally thousands of women in fitness and figure control programs have taught us that the data on this chart accurately reflect the figure most sought after by today's woman.

A Final Note

Now you are ready to set some realistic goals for yourself. While taking into account your time schedule and eating habits, give thought to establishing new habits for healthy living. Once you have begun a program of exercise, stick with it—and keep your goals in mind.

Recommended References

De Vries, Herbert A. *Physiology of Exercise.* 2d ed. Dubuque, Iowa: Wm. C. Brown, 1974.

Guyton, Arthur C. *Function of the Human Body.* Philadelphia: W. B. Saunders, 1969.

Karpovich, Peter V., and Sinning, Wayne E. *Physiology of Muscular Activity.* Philadelphia: W. B. Saunders, 1971.

Mathews, Donald K., and Fox, Edward L. *The Physiological Basis of Physical Education and Athletics.* Philadelphia: W. B. Saunders, 1971.

Tuttle, W. W., and Schottelius, Byron A. *Textbook of Physiology.* St. Louis: C. V. Mosby, 1969.

WARM-UP AND WARM-DOWN

*Even as airplane engines must be tuned
up before taking off, so must a human
being have a tuning up process. The
body has many miles of blood vessels
and nerves to stimulate, if you want
to travel in high gear.*

— Norman Vincent Peale

WARM-UP

Warming up your body to prepare for more strenuous exercise is vitally important in the prevention of muscular injury and severe muscle soreness. In order to
warm-up the muscles properly, begin your exercise program gradually with the
light stretching exercises described in this chapter. Slowly increase the pace and
intensity of the exercises until your body begins to feel loose and warm. Perspiration is an excellent indication that your muscles are indeed warm and ready to
endure more intense exercise. Since each person is at a different level of fitness,
the amount of time spent warming up will vary with each person. Some persons

37

will need at least fifteen minutes of warm-up; others will require more time; and a few can get by on less.

We have already said that perspiration is a good indication of your readiness to take more strenuous exercise. Perspiration occurs when your normal body temperature rises because of the increase in blood and muscle temperatures. This increase is important in order to prepare your muscles properly so that you are less likely to sustain injury or severe soreness. Because the flexibility, endurance, and strength exercises place considerable stress on the muscles, we cannot emphasize strongly enough the importance of a warm-up.

Aside from the prevention of severe muscle soreness and injury, a thorough warm-up brings other benefits. For instance, since the blood and muscle temperatures have been increased, the functioning of muscles improves, and this will enable you to benefit more from your exercise. Also, the processes which help burn calories are increased during a warm-up, and the burning of calories is what you want in weight loss.

WARM–DOWN

You would not stop an automobile by running it at seventy miles an hour into a brick wall; instead, you anticipate and begin braking gradually until you come to a complete halt. By the same token you should warm down the body in the same way that you warm up, with a gradual change in the tempo of activity. By using light stretching exercises you will begin to slow the pace naturally, allowing the body to cool off.

During vigorous activity the muscles assist the circulation of blood. If all activity stops abruptly the effect could be a pooling of blood in the extremities, which might result in muscle cramps or sudden blacking out.[1] This is why it is just as important to include a warm-down in your exercise program as it is to include a warm-up. One suggestion for a good ending: sitting down, slowly rotate your head around, rotate from side to side, and finally just let your head hang forward. Now would be a good time for your relaxation (see Chapter Ten).

EXERCISES

Rope jumping, running in place, bench stepping, hopping, and skipping are all excellent exercises to start the blood circulation in preparation for exercise. Light stretching exercises further insure against muscle injury and soreness. Many of the flexibility exercises can be used in warm-up and warm-down by lightly stretching instead of holding a static stretch (Chapter Nine). Remember

---

[1] H. A. de Vries, *Physiology of Exercise* (Dubuque, Iowa: Wm. C. Brown, 1974), p. 138.

to concentrate on warming up the whole body and not just a portion of it. It is important to do a Lateral Side Bend and Standing Waist Twist before bending forward, as in touching the toes, in order to release the muscles of the back so as to not injure them.[2]

The following are examples of the types of exercises that can be used for light stretching when warming up or warming down:

1. Side Bend.	(Included in Chapter Seven, p. 49. Use the same exercise with light stretching.)
2. Standing Waist Twist.	(Included in Chapter Seven, p. 50. Use the same exercise with light stretching.)
3. Overhead Stretch.	Standing, feet together, hands and arms overhead. Reach with one hand as high as possible as if to touch a star. Reach slowly with other hand. Repeat total exercise several times.
4. Toe Touch.	Standing, feet together. Bend forward from the waist and try to touch toes with hands. Repeat slowly several times.
5. Gravity Hang.	Standing, feet shoulder-width apart. Bend forward from the waist and hang. Pretend you are a rag doll. The force of gavity pulls the upper body down. You should feel a pull in the back of your legs.
6. Sitting Long Stretch.	(Included in Chapter Nine, p. 78. Use the same exercise with light stretching.)
7. Wide Stride Stretch.	(Included in Chapter Nine, p. 78. Use the same exercise with light stretching.)

---

[2] F. W. Kasch and J. L. Boyer, *Adult Fitness* (Palo Alto: National Press Books, 1968), p. 43.

THE FIGURE EXERCISE – STRENGTH

*Health and fitness are better than any
gold, and bodily vigour than boundless prosperity.*

— Ecclesiasticus XXX:15
(The Apocrypha)

Muscular strength refers to the ability to exert force or overcome resistance. The muscles must contract to push, pull, lift, or work against resistance. This is what strength exercises are all about—working your muscles against resistance and therefore firming, tightening, and contouring them. Just as men perform strength-building exercises to develop their bodies, you will find that the same strength-building exercises will contour your female figure.

The two types of resistance exercises are isometrics and isotonics. Using one of these types of strength exercises, or a combination of the two, increases the strength of the muscle. Pushing, pulling, or lifting a resistance is called isotonic exercise. An example of an isotonic exercise would be a push-up, since the muscles involved have to push or lift the weight of the body; the body is acting as the resistance. Isometric exercises involve working against an immovable or controlled resistance; such a resistance could be created by pushing both hands together with equal force, therefore contracting the muscles, and holding the exercise until the muscles begin to quiver.

Currently, the best form of resistance exercise is weight training, which in most cases is isotonic exercise because you are pushing, lifting, or pulling a resistance. However, isokinetic machines are now being researched and developed and when these machines can be marketed at a reasonable price they should revolutionize the field of weight training. They are designed to adjust constantly to the muscle contraction of the user and to give optimal resistance whatever the angle of pull. Weight training is an excellent form of strength exercise because it offers a quick and easy way to overload the muscles. (Overload was discussed in Chapter Five.) In order to develop greater strength, which is also the key to contouring, muscles must be challenged to work against a greater resistance once they have become adjusted to a particular load.

Since most persons do not have easy access to complex weight training equipment, the strength exercises in the first part of this chapter are ones that use the body's own weight as the primary resistance; thus they can be performed easily at home. However, if you wish to purchase ankle, wrist, and waist weight-belts to supplement your strength program it will bring results more quickly. (The ankle, wrist, and waist weight-belts do not reduce those specific areas, of course; their purpose is to add load to the limb or total body, and thus increase the work of the muscles.) Many other items found in the home can be used as weights, such as large books, canned goods, ski boots, heavy wrenches, irons, pots and pans, or plastic bleach bottles filled with sand.

DEVELOPING A PROGRAM

As you begin to develop a strength exercise program it is important to maintain a balance of exercises. Even though you may feel that one particular part of your body needs more emphasis than another, the key to a good shape is to first balance the exercises for all parts of the body, then add extra exercises for problem areas. This chapter contains many exercises grouped to serve different areas of the body.* Start your program by taking a look at your time schedule and then selecting as many exercises from each body area as your time will allow. List these exercises on a sheet of paper, then make a chart like the one below (see also Appendix, Chart 4). Repeat each exercise as many times as you can. When each exercise has been completed, record the number of repetitions on the chart. Each time you exercise (work out) try to increase your number of

---

* We shall not recommend any facial-contortion exercises, because some cosmetic surgeons argue that such exercises can cause unnecessary wrinkling. It should be noted that exercises for the upper body also exercise the muscles of the face.

repetitions for each exercise. When your exercises begin to take too much time to perform, add a weight load using one of the items mentioned above. The load will allow you to perform fewer repetitions, thus making your exercise time shorter.

EXERCISE	NUMBER OF REPETITIONS								
	DATE								
	6/1	6/3	6/5	6/9	6/11				
1. Standing waist twist	25	30	30	36					
2. Arm fling	15	18	20	20					
3. Standing leg lift	16	17	18	19					
4. Side bend	20	24	24	24					
5. Sitting ankle flexion & extension	30	35	36	40					
6. Pop-ups	12	12	13	14					
7. Kneeling leg lift series	10	12	13	13					
8. Let-down	4	7	8	8					

STRENGTH GROUP I

NECK, SHOULDERS, UPPER ARMS, AND UPPER BACK

 *HEAD LIFT*

Position: Lie on back with arms at side.

Action: Lift head (only) as high as possible and return to starting position. Repeat at a steady pace.

Position and Action

 *PUSH–UP*

Position: Assume prone position supported on hands and toes with body absolutely straight. Keep body straight throughout exercise.

Action: Lower body to two to six inches from floor and push back to starting position. Repeat at a steady pace.

Position for exercises 2 and 3   *Action for exercises 2 and 3*

LET DOWN

(An alternate for the push-up. To be done until you can push up.)

Position: Same as above.

Action: Lower body as slowly as possible until you can no longer hold body in horizontal position. Return to starting position any way you can. Repeat.

 ARM FLING

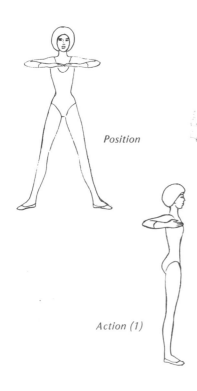

Position

Action (1)

Position: Stand, feet apart, arms at shoulder level in front of shoulders with elbows bent.

Action: (1) Fling bent elbows as far behind body as possible while keeping arms at shoulder level.
(2) Return to starting position and fling arms straight backward, try to touch hands at shoulder level. Return to (1) and repeat exercise (alternate steps 1 and 2). Use a fast pace.

Action (2)

5 ARM CIRCLES

Position and Action

Position: Stand, feet apart, arms extended to the sides of body at shoulder level.

Action: (1) Rotate arms forward in a large circular motion. Rotate from large circles to small circles. (2) Same exercise as (1) with backward rotation. Repeat at a steady pace.

STRENGTH GROUP II

ABDOMINALS AND WAISTLINE

6 POP-UP

Position and Action

Position: Lie on back (supine), knees bent, feet secured,* head raised off floor with chin touching chest, back rounded, arms folded across chest.

Action: Curl the upper body just a few inches off the floor and return to starting position. Use a fast pace.

---

*To secure feet, have someone hold them down; or place them under a heavy object such as a low sofa.

ISOLATED SIT–UP

Position: Lie on back (supine), knees bent, feet up on a chair or other object that is approximately 20 inches high and allows feet to be secured. Head should be raised off floor with chin touching chest, back rounded, arms folded across the chest.

Action: Curl the upper body just a few inches off the floor and return to starting position. Use a fast pace.

Position and Action

 KNEE TO NOSE SIT–UP

Position

Position: Lie on back (supine) with arms extended overhead.

Action: Raise leg (leg straight) and at the same time raise upper body to sitting position. Grasp leg with hands (as close to ankle as possible) and try to touch knee with nose. No rest between sit-ups. Repeat on opposite leg. Use a steady pace.

Action

 *JACK KNIFE SIT–UP*

Position: Lie on back (supine) with arms extended overhead.

Position

Action: Raise both legs (legs straight) and at the same time raise upper body to sitting position. Touch toes with fingers while in pike position. Use a steady pace.

Action

 WIDE STRIDE SIT–UP

Position: Lie on back (supine) with arms extended overhead and legs in stride position (knees about two feet apart).

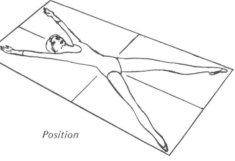

Action: (1) Raise torso to sitting position and reach with both arms toward left foot. Lie down. Use a steady pace. (2) Raise torso and reach straight forward between legs. Repeat (1) but reach for right foot.

Position

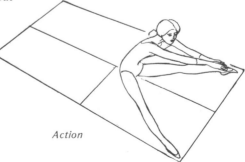

Action

SCOOP

Position: Sit with knees bent, legs together close to chest, feet off floor, and hands on floor behind body for support.

Action: (1) Extend legs three inches from floor. (2) Lift legs straight up to extended V position. Return to starting position. Repeat at a steady pace. (An alternate position is with upper body resting on elbows throughout exercise. Use this position until you can accomplish the regular position.)

Position   Action (1)   Action (2)

 V–SIT

Position: Same as extended V position in exercise 11.

Action: Slowly raise and lower legs. Repeat at a steady pace.

Position   Action

TWISTING SIT-UP

Position: Lie on back (supine), knees bent, feet secured,* head up with chin touching chest, back rounded, arms folded across chest.

Action: Use pop-up exercise and twist to alternate sides while sitting up. Repeat at a fast pace.

Position

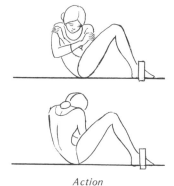

Action

 SIDE BEND

Position: Stand, feet apart, one arm circled overhead and one circled downward in front of body.

Action: Keep body and hips in vertical alignment and bend as far to one side as possible. Exchange arms and repeat movement to other side. Use a fast pace.

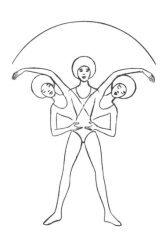

Position and Action

---

* To secure feet, have someone hold them, or place them under a low, heavy object such as a sofa.

STANDING WAIST TWIST

Position: Stand with legs apart and arms at shoulder level in front of shoulders with elbows bent.

Action: Keep body straight from waist down. Turn upper body (including head) as far as possible to the right, then as far as possible to the left (alternate directions). Arms must be held at shoulder level with elbows bent. Repeat at a fast pace.

Position   *Action*

 SITTING WAIST TWIST

Position: Sit with legs straight and toes pointed. Support body by placing hands on floor at sides.

Action: Roll from one side to the other (over buttocks). Palms must remain on floor. Repeat at a fast pace. (This is an exercise that has been done incorrectly and has been said to reduce the size of the hips, which is false.)

Position

Action

STRENGTH GROUP III

HIPS, LOWER BACK, AND THIGHS

 HIP-LIFT

Position: Lie on back (supine) with knees bent and arms at side.

Action: Lift hips as high as possible, leaving shoulders and feet on floor. Return to starting position. Use a steady pace.

Position   *Action*

 SEAT-LIFT LEG EXTENSION

Position: Assume crab position—body supported on feet and hands, knees bent, seat on floor.

Action: (1) Lift seat. (2) Lift and extend leg. (3) Return leg to floor. (4) Return seat to starting position, and repeat using other leg. Use a steady pace.

Position and Action (4)   *Actions (1) and (3)*   *Action (2)*

SIDE–LYING LEG LIFTS

Position: Lie on side, support body on hands, with arm and upper body straight.

Action: (1) Lift one leg up to side of body; then behind body; then in front of body. Alternate sides by rolling on buttocks and using other leg. Use a steady pace. (2) Hold top leg high, lift bottom leg to meet top leg. Alternate sides. Use a steady pace.

Position and Action (1)

Position and Action (2)

 SIDE–LYING DOUBLE LEG SWING

Position: Lie on side, both hands in front of body for support, upper body straight, legs raised off floor, and toes pointed.

Action: Swing both legs in front of body to opposite side in same position. Keep legs straight and off floor through the swinging movement. (Arms must be lifted for legs to pass in front of body.) Repeat at a steady pace.

Position and Action

SWAN

Position: Lie prone (face down) with arms and legs extended.

Action: Lift chest, arms, and legs off floor. Hold in upward position. Repeat at a steady pace.

Position and Action

KNEELING LEG–LIFT SERIES

Position

Action (1)

Position: Down on hands and knees.

Action: (1) Extend leg to side, keep leg straight. Touch toe to floor and raise upward as far as possible. Head up. Repeat at a steady pace. (2) Extend leg to rear, lift straight leg, bend knee behind head, and straighten leg again at a steady pace. Keep head up. Repeat. (3) Extend leg to rear, lift leg as high as possible, drop leg down, and bend knee forward, bringing knee to chest and dropping head to meet knee. Repeat at a steady pace.

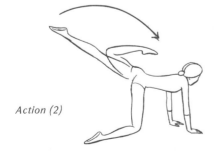

Action (2)

Action (3)

STRIDE LEG CROSS–OVER

Position: Assume a supine position (lying face up), body extended, resting (off floor) on heels, upper body supported on hands (arms straight) and legs apart.

Action: Cross one leg over the other (legs straight and seat lifted) turning body as you cross. Touch toe as far to one side of body as possible and return to starting position. Repeat on opposite side. Use a steady pace.

Position   *Action*

 STANDING LEG–LIFTS

Position: Stand resting one hand on back of chair (or similar item) for balance with weight on inside leg (next to chair), knee bent slightly. Outside leg is held slightly behind and to side of body, leg straight and pointed toe resting lightly on floor.

Position and Action (1)

Action: (1) Lift outside leg to the side as high as possible, lower to floor and repeat. Use a steady pace. (2) Lift outside leg to the rear as high as possible, lower to floor and repeat. Use a steady pace. (3) Lift outside leg to the front as high as possible, lower to floor and repeat. Use a steady pace. (Body must remain upright. Use correct posture, with head held high. Use arm position shown. Repeat exercises on both sides of body.)

Position and Action (2)

Position and Action (3)

 SLIMMER BOUNCE

Position: Assume a stride position, with knees bent, feet angled outward, back straight, and arms to side of body at shoulder level.

Action: Lower and raise seat in an up-and-down motion, keeping knees bent at all times. (The feet must be at least two feet apart with knees angled the same as the feet. The knees must remain directly over the feet at all times. The seat must not drop below the knees. The body position is similar to that of sitting in a straight-back chair.)

Position

Action

STRENGTH GROUP IV

CALVES AND ANKLES

 HEEL RAISES

Position: Standing, feet apart, arms to side of body at shoulder level.

Action: Raise heels up as far as possible (on toes). Repeat with feet parallel, angled out, and angled in. Use a slow pace.

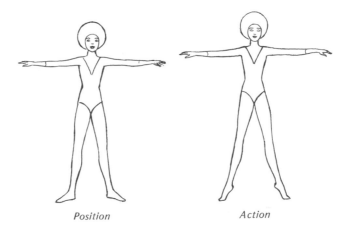

Position   *Action*

 SITTING ANKLE FLEXION AND EXTENSION

Position: Sit with legs straight, support body by placing hands on floor at sides.

Action: Extend toes forward as far as possible, then pull toes back as far as possible. Repeat at a fast pace.

Position and Action

WEIGHT TRAINING

Weight training—or resistance exercise, as it is sometimes called—is the most efficient exercise for contouring the figure. If procedures are followed carefully, results are experienced quickly and the effect is long-lasting. Because weight training is so valuable to figure contouring, this portion of the strength chapter was included to give essential information and exercises to those interested in starting a weight training program.

EQUIPMENT FOR HOME USE

The simple pieces of equipment shown here are inexpensive and may be conveniently used at home. The exercises described and pictured in the rest of this chapter show how to use this equipment for figure contouring.

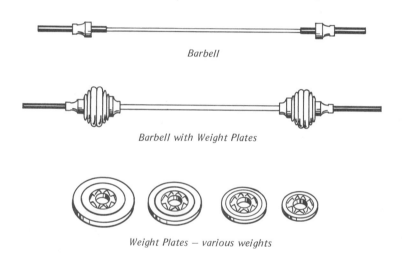

Barbell

Barbell with Weight Plates

Weight Plates — various weights

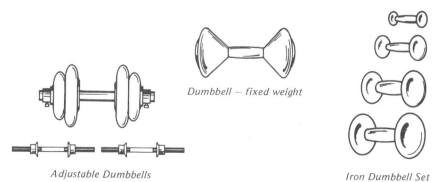

Dumbbell — fixed weight

Adjustable Dumbbells

Iron Dumbbell Set

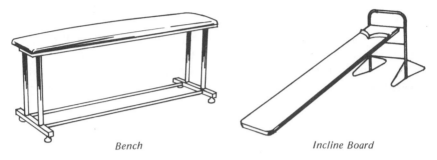

Bench   *Incline Board*

The weight training equipment shown here is available in most gyms and salons. The size and cost of most of this equipment make it impractical for home use.

Rowing Machine

Stall Bars   *Non–Adjustable Barbells and Rack*

Flexion–Extension Table

Multiple Station Gym Machine

Stationary Bicycle

Wall Pulley

Supine Press Bench with Rack

Treadmill

Lat Machine

The System to Use

For all practical purposes, the simple "set system" of weight training is the most effective method for you. A set consists of a certain number of repetitions of a single exercise; in a simple set system, all of the sets of a given exercise are performed before moving on to the next exercise. For example, two sets of eight repetitions means that you do a given exercise eight times, rest for about one minute, and then do the same exercise again eight times. Repetitions should be performed without interruption, using a pace not too fast and not too slow.

A Graduated Program

There are many types of weight training programs. With proper supervision, a program can be individualized and made much more technical. The graduated program described here is a basic one—effective and simple to follow.

Program I:	One set, 15 to 20 repetitions
Program II:	Two sets, 10 to 15 repetitions
Program III:	Three sets, 5 to 10 repetitions

Follow Program I for approximately six weeks, working out three times a week and using the resistance progression described below. Then begin Program II and complete the same procedure before moving on to Program III.

Resistance Progression

Resistance refers to the load or the amount of weight being used in an exercise. The proper load for each individual differs for each exercise, since some persons are naturally stronger than others. The simplest method of determining the correct resistance for each exercise is old-fashioned trial and error. Just pick a weight you think you can handle without much strain. If you can't use it to complete the number of assigned sets and repetitions of an exercise, it's too heavy. The next time you work out, select a weight that seems light enough to permit you to complete the exercise. Make a chart like the one shown below (see also Appendix, Chart 5), and keep a record of the changes made in your program as illustrated.

Muscles will adjust to a certain load, so it is necessary to increase the resistance after you can easily complete the designated number of sets and repetitions of an exercise. Remember, here you do not increase the number of repetitions or sets; increase the resistance instead. This overload is vital in achieving the greater strength required for figure contouring.

Number of Exercises

Every program should include exercises for each area of the body. An ideal program will include at least 15 to 20 exercises, with more exercises to be added

PROGRAM I	SETS One	REPETITIONS 15								
EXERCISE	FOR	CHANGES								
		DATE								
		6/15	6/17	6/19	6/21	6/23	6/25	6/27	6/29	6/31
1. Arm Curls	Arms	10 lbs.	10 lbs.	10 lbs.	12 lbs.	12 lbs.	15 lbs.	15 lbs.	15 lbs.	20 lbs.
2.										
3.										
4.										
5.										
6.										
7.										
8.										

for problem areas. In order to minimize fatigue, avoid doing consecutive exercises for the same part of the body. The length of time to spend on a workout depends on the number of exercises in your program. A good workout will take from one to two hours.

Performing the Exercise

Correct posture is important, regardless of the exercise position. For example, when standing keep your body straight and your feet about a shoulder-width apart, with your knees unlocked; when sitting keep your shoulders directly over your hips; when lying down on your back, pull your abdomen in and try to hold your back flat against the bench. During all exercises, don't forget to breathe regularly. The two most common grips, and the ones that will be used for the following exercises, are the over-grip and under-grip, as shown in Figure 7-2.

Over-Grip

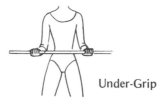
Under-Grip

Fig. 7-2.

WEIGHT TRAINING GROUP I

NECK, SHOULDERS, UPPER ARMS, UPPER BACK, CHEST, AND SIDES

 WRIST CURLS, under-grip

Rest forearms on thighs and flex wrists upward as far as possible.

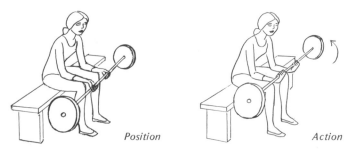

Position   *Action*

 ARM CURLS, under-grip

With arms fully extended bend arms bringing weight to chest.

Position   *Action*

TRICEPS PRESS, over-grip

With arms extended overhead, lower bar as close to the back of the head as possible.

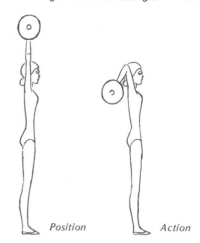

Position   *Action*

 ROWING, over-grip

With hands close together bring bar upward to chin keeping elbows high.

 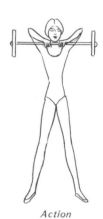

Position   *Action*

 SUPINE LATERAL RAISES, under-grip

Raise arms upward above chest with arms extended.

Position and Action

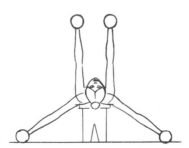

BENCH PRESS, over-grip

Support bar over chest and extend
arms upward.

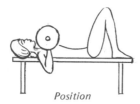

Position   *Action*

 OVERHEAD PRESS, over-grip

Lift bar overhead until arms are
fully extended.

Position   *Action*

 PRONE LATERAL RAISES, over-grip

Bring arms upward as far as possible.

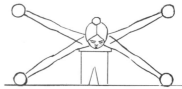

Position and Action

WEIGHT TRAINING GROUP II

ABDOMINALS AND WAISTLINE

 SIT-UP

The higher the elevation of the incline board, the more difficult the sit-up.

Position and Action

 DUMBELL SIDE-BEND, over-grip

Bend to one side as far as possible and then to the other side. Keep feet together.

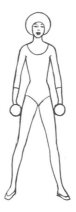 

Position   *Action*

BARBELL WAIST TWIST, over-grip

With barbell resting on shoulders, turn upper body as far in one direction as possible. Alternate directions. As a safety precaution use care with heavier weight.

Position   *Action*

 BARBELL SIDE–BEND, over-grip

With bar resting on shoulders, bend as far to one side as possible and then to the other. Be careful with heavier weights.

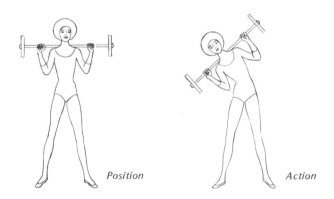

Position   *Action*

LEG RAISES, *ankle weights*

With arms overhead grasping end of board, bring knees to chest, extend legs upward and lower.

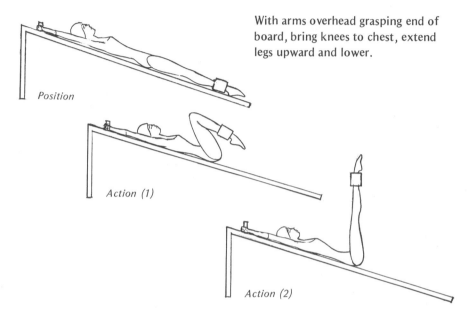

Position

Action (1)

Action (2)

 HIP FLEXOR, *over-grip*

Hanging from a horizontal bar, bring knees up to chest, using ankle weights.

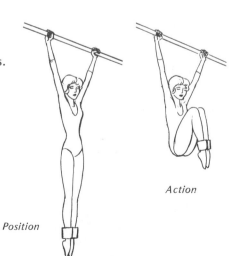

Action

Position

WEIGHT TRAINING GROUP III

HIPS, LOWER BACK, THIGHS, CALVES, AND ANKLES

 DEADLIFT, over-grip

Lift bar and assume a standing position.

Position

Action

 HACK LIFT, over-grip

Lift bar and assume a standing position.

Position

Action

LEG RAISES, side, rear, and front, with ankle weights

Standing erect, raise leg upward as far as possible. Do not kick leg. Do each position as a separate exercise.

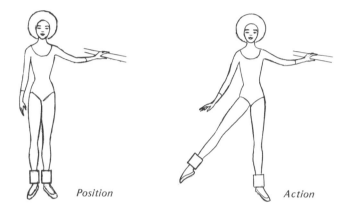

Position   *Action*

 HEEL RAISES, over-grip

With bar resting on shoulders, raise heels off floor as far as possible. Do in three positions: with toes pointed inward, outward, and parallel.

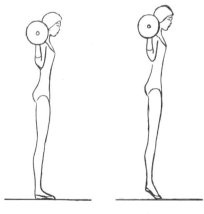

Position   *Action*

ONE–HALF SQUAT, over-grip

With bar resting on shoulders, squat as if sitting on the edge of a chair.

Position   *Action*

 STANDING FORWARD BEND, over-grip

With bar resting on shoulders, bend forward keeping back straight.

Position   *Action*

THE LIFE EXERCISE – ENDURANCE

May you live all the days of your life!

— Jonathan Swift

The heart is one of the truly vital mechanisms in the body, because all of our life's processes depend on it. The heart must pump nutrient- and oxygen-carrying blood to all the organs and tissues of the body through a complex network of arteries, veins, and capillaries, and at the same time it must assist all the other vital organs in performing their functions: if it fails, the entire organism fails. The heart is a muscle, and like other muscles it needs exercise to be healthy and operate efficiently.

For most of our grandmothers or great-grandmothers, an ordinary day's work included a great deal of physical activity. Cast iron pots and wooden buckets of water were heavy to lift, wood floors were hard to clean, and clothes had to be washed and scrubbed by hand. It used to be that a woman needed rest after working all day. Now what most of us really need when we come home from work is to get out the jogging shoes or the bicycle and exercise!

We must remember that in one respect our bodies are similar to

71

machines—when they are not used, they rust and cease to function. Is your heart slowly rusting away? Consider these words from Dr. Jean Mayer: "The explosion of coronary heart disease is so sudden in terms of generations and so widespread that it can only be called a 'new epidemic.' With heart attacks striking down younger and younger people, it's obvious that a beneficial regimen of exercise and diet is a must for the young person."[1]

THE TYPES OF ACTIVITY

Although strength and flexibility exercises have specific benefits for the muscles and joints of your body, they do very little to stimulate the heart and the circulatory and respiratory systems. The type of exercise that does this is endurance exercise, and is also referred to as cardiovascular, cardiorespiratory, or aerobic exercise.[2] It is the kind of exercise that increases your pulse rate during the activity, causes you to perspire and breathe heavily, and in general invigorates your entire body. The most common endurance activities are:

jogging	jumping rope	stair-climbing
fast walking	swimming	(bench-stepping)
running in place	bicycling	

THE PULSE RATE

The pulse rate is the all-important indicator in endurance exercise. There are three pulse rates that you need to be aware of: your resting pulse rate, your active pulse rate, and your recovery pulse rate.

1.   *The resting pulse rate* is an indication of your normal heartbeat; it is your pulse taken after you have been sitting quietly for at least ten minutes. Endurance exercise is designed to strengthen the heart and *lower the resting pulse rate,* because a strong heart can accomplish its task with fewer pumping actions or beats. Therefore, when your resting pulse rate begins to lower, you will know that your endurance exercise is working. To give you an example, Roger Bannister, the first man to run a mile in less than four minutes, lowered his resting pulse rate from the high seventies to the low forties. It is not uncommon for a cross-country runner to have a resting pulse rate in the thirties.

---

[1] Jean Mayer, "Prime Target for a Heart Attack," *Family Health Magazine* (New York), vol. 4, no. 8 (August 1972), pp. 37–38.

[2] "Cardiovascular" in Fred W. Kasch and John L. Boyer, *Adult Fitness* (Palo Alto: National Press Books, 1968), p. 44; "Cardiorespiratory" in Donald K. Mathews and Edward L. Fox, *The Physiological Basis of Physical Education and Athletics* (Philadelphia: W. B. Saunders, 1971), p. 68; "Aerobic" in Kenneth H. Cooper, *The New Aerobics* (New York: Bantam Books, 1970), p. 15.

2. *The active pulse rate* is taken during activity and indicates the extent of your exercise. We have learned that in order to lower the resting pulse rate, we must increase the pulse rate during activity. Your pulse rate will increase as you exercise, so you must check it at various intervals during your activity. Take a few moments to stop and count your pulse, then continue your exercise until you reach the maximum pulse rate (MPR) for your age group (see below).

3. *The recovery pulse rate* is very important, and one that you should not forget, because it tells you if your activity has been too strenuous. The recovery pulse should be taken approximately thirty minutes after finishing your workout and should be taken in the same manner as the resting pulse (after you have been sitting quietly for at least ten minutes). This pulse count should be very close to your resting pulse count. If your pulse rate at this time is still high (roughly, more than five beats higher than your resting pulse) your activity has been too strenuous and you should reduce the intensity of the exercise at your next session.

How to Count Your Pulse

The best method of taking your pulse is at the arteries on either side of the neck. Place your fingers, *not* your thumb, on one side of the Adam's apple, then move them slightly until you can feel a pulsebeat. Use the second hand of a watch or clock to count the number of beats in fifteen seconds, then multiply by four and you will have your number of beats per minute.

THE MAXIMUM PULSE RATE (MPR) SYSTEM

The MPR system is designed for those who are just beginning an endurance program, and we suggest that as you improve your level of endurance you investigate Dr. Kenneth Cooper's Aerobic system.[3] You will want to use an activity that increases your heartbeat rather rapidly, since the amount of time you can spend in exercise will probably be limited. Use the following table to determine what your maximum pulse rate should be during activity.

AGE	MPR
15–30	180
31–40	170
41–50	160
51–60	150
61–70	140
71+	130

[3] Cooper, *The New Aerobics.*

Don't attempt to reach your MPR the first time out; instead, work to increase your pulse rate gradually, until after a few weeks of activity you are able to work to your maximum pulse rate. In the beginning, you should end your workout when you are tired, and record your active pulse rate at that point. Later, when you can continue until your MPR is reached, you will end your workout at that point. From then on, each time you work out, continue the activity until your maximum pulse rate is reached.

The Importance of Exercising Regularly

In order to lower the resting pulse rate, you must continue your program of endurance exercises on a regular basis. The exercises should be done at least three times per week and more often if possible: every day would not be too much. Keep in mind that an added advantage of this type of exercise is that it helps burn calories more rapidly than almost any other type of exercise. This means that if you need to lose weight, you won't have to cut down so much on your food intake if you do endurance exercises faithfully.

An important note: If you have had relatively little activity or exercise in the past few years, we suggest you undergo a complete medical checkup by a licensed physician before starting this program.

THE YOUTH EXERCISE – FLEXIBILITY

I shall grow old but never lose life's zest,
Because the road's last turn will be the best.

— Henry Van Dyke

Flexibility is the quality of being pliant, versatile, and adaptable to change. We have called flexibility exercise the "youth exercise" because it combats the effects of aging on the range of movement of our joints. With age, our bodies tend to become restricted in the actions of bending, stretching, and reaching which came easily to us in our youth. If we were to return to the school playground and attempt to go through the motions of the past, most of us would be unable to perform the antics and movements of our early youth. This is indication enough of our loss of flexibility.

Flexibility exercises are designed to alleviate inflexibility caused by shortened muscles and ligaments as discussed in Chapter Five. Flexibility exercises stretch the muscles that need stretching, allowing us to have more freedom in our movement and enabling us to work more efficiently. This freedom to move, to reach and bend without restriction, will also provide a feeling of youthfulness,

75

which many of us feel we have lost, and an appearance of youthfulness as well. If we feel young physically and mentally, we can approach aging with a more positive outlook.

Many of the aches and pains associated with old age are caused simply by inflexibility in the joints. Muscles drawn so tightly that they ache can soon become a source of chronic pain. Flexibility exercises, by eliminating the source of the problem, can ease many of our aches and pains. Furthermore, if our joints are flexible, many strains and sprains can be avoided; in this respect, flexibility exercises help prevent serious injury.

GENERAL INFORMATION ABOUT FLEXIBILITY EXERCISES

Care should be taken before beginning the exercises included in this chapter. So read and heed the following information.

Warm–up

Since flexibility exercises place great stress on the muscles, it is extremely important that you take an adequate warm-up before your workout. Try to spend at least ten minutes warming up before attempting a static stretch position.

Static Stretch

Two common techniques are used in flexibility exercise: the dynamic stretch and the static stretch. The first method is not recommended. It is called dynamic or ballistic stretching because it involves bouncing, bobbing, and jerky movements. The dynamic method stimulates the stretch reflex, which was discussed in Chapter Five, and inhibits the stretching of the muscle that needs to be made flexible. In addition, it often causes unnecessarily severe muscle soreness.[1] We believe the best method for increasing flexibility is static stretching, which involves holding muscle groups in a stretched position for a recommended period of time. This method counteracts the stretch reflex and allows for relaxation of the muscle fibers.[2] In order to achieve the desired results from flexibility exercise, try to hold each position for 15 seconds, and as you progress, work up to a maximum hold of *at least one minute.*

Positions

As you begin the exercises described in this chapter, most of you will not at first be able to achieve many of the positions shown. In every such case, begin with

---

[1] H. A. De Vries, *Physiology of Exercise* (Dubuque, Iowa: Wm. C. Brown, 1974), p. 437.

[2] De Vries, *Physiology of Exercise*, p. 434.

whatever position your level of flexibility will allow, and each time you exercise attempt to come closer and closer to the prescribed position. Remember not to bounce in order to achieve a position; instead, pull slowly and hold each position without moving. Mastering both the position and the maximum hold will take time, so be patient. You will find that some exercises will be easier than others. Don't cheat yourself by eliminating a difficult exercise from your program.

EXERCISES

Hips

One of our most common problems is inflexibility of the hip joint, which makes it difficult to achieve the correct position in the sitting exercises. Generally most people cannot angle the hips forward while in a sitting position and if these exercises are done incorrectly, they will be of little benefit. For example, in the sitting long stretch we usually sit with the hips tilted backward, the back rounded, and the head down as shown in Figure 9-1. To correct this assume the position in Figure 9-2 by keeping the back absolutely straight, the chin up, and most important, the hips angled forward. One of the best ways to correct this common occurrence is to think "belly button down, head up." Concentrate on angling the hips forward, keeping a straight, almost arched back with your chin and your head up while keeping your eyes fixed on a spot or object in front of you. The minute you allow the hips to tilt backward, while rounding the back, you lose the benefit of the exercise.

Figure 9-1    Figure 9-2

FLEXIBILITY GROUP I

HIPS

 SITTING LONG STRETCH

Position: Sit with legs together and straight, keep back straight, hips tilted forward with hands grasping ankles.

Action: (1) With feet pointed, pull body forward while keeping chin up and neck stretched. Attempt to touch your belly button to your thighs. Hold position. (2) Repeat same exercise with feet flexed.

Position

Action

 WIDE STRIDE STRETCH

Position: Sit with legs apart, hips tilted forward, and back straight. Determining how far apart the legs should be depends upon each individual's level of flexibility. If the knees bend during the exercise the legs are too far apart. Work to widen the stride as you progress.

Action: (1) With feet pointed, grasp as far down one leg as possible, pull body forward while keeping chin up and neck stretched. Attempt to touch your belly button to your thigh. Repeat to the front with one hand grasping each ankle. Then repeat action on the other leg. (2) Repeat same three actions with feet flexed.

Position

Action (1)

Action (2)

FROG STRETCH

Position: Sit with knees bent outward and soles of feet together. With elbows out grasp feet while keeping chin up, hips forward and back straight. In the maximum position the knees should be flat on the floor with the heels of the feet touching the crotch.

Position

Action: Pull body forward with chin up and neck stretched. Attempt to touch your belly button to your feet.

Action

STANDING BEND OR STRETCH

Position (1). Stand with feet slightly apart, knees bent and hands on floor in front of toes. The distance between the hands and feet will vary depending on your flexibility. The more flexible you are, the closer the hands will be to the feet.

Position (1)   *Action (1)*

Action (1). Straighten legs and hold position without bending knees. When this position can be held for maximum time, move on to position 2.

Position (2). Stand with knees bent, grasping ankles behind heels with elbows behind knees.

Action (2). Straighten legs and hold. Try to pull chest to knees.

Position (2)   *Action (2)*

FLEXIBILITY GROUP II

BACK

 PRETZEL

Position: Lie on back with arms at side.

Action: Raise legs overhead until balls of the feet are resting on the floor as close to the head as possible while keeping legs straight. Do not let the knees bend. As you progress, move the feet closer to the head.

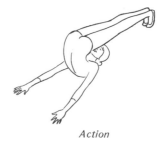

Action

 PRONE ARCH

Position: Lie prone (face down) with hands on floor directly beneath chest.

Action: Lift upper body with arms, bend legs at knee while pointing feet toward head. Arch back attempting to bring feet and head as close together as possible. Keep thighs and pelvis on the floor.

Action

BACK ARCH

Action

Position: Lie on back with arms overhead, elbows bent, and hands on floor. Bend knees with feet on floor close to seat.

Action: Lift body while extending elbows and knees, arch back, and tilt head back. Work toward achieving a high back arch and moving hands and feet closer together. It might be wise to have a partner help lift you the first few times.

FLEXIBILITY GROUP III

SHOULDERS AND ANKLES

SHOULDER STRETCH

Position: Stand clasping hands behind back with arms straight.

Action: (1) Raise arms as high as possible without leaning forward. Keep a straight vertical position. As you progress, have a partner raise your arms higher, because it will be impossible, after a point, for you to do so on your own. (2) Bend forward at the waist and bring clasped hands overhead. The force of gravity will aid in pulling the arms downward.

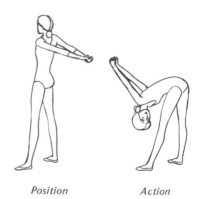

Position   *Action*

ANKLE STRETCH

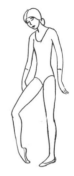

Position: Stand resting weight on one foot; roll opposite foot forward and over so that full sole is exposed, then carefully apply weight to the top of the foot.

Action: Gradually place more and more weight on the foot. Repeat on opposite foot.

Position and Action

THE SANITY EXERCISE - RELAXATION

Go placidly among the noise and haste
and remember what peace there may be
in silence.

— Max Ehrmann

We have mentioned the relationship of the mind and body throughout our book. In no other exercise do they work together as closely as in the conscious process of relaxation. Relaxation is time given to renew and refresh our strengths—physical, mental, and emotional. We call relaxation the sanity exercise because of the calming effect it has on our lives. No matter what life brings, we are able to face it with less fatigue, and evaluate the consequences of our actions with better judgment, when our minds are relaxed and decisions are not made in haste.

Exercising our powers of relaxation has become necessary to offset the fast pace of living and the pressures of time, which are constantly undermining our own mental organization. The psychological difficulty in keeping up with today's changing values and patterns of living is taking its toll on our energies.

The sharp rise in emotional illness in America today is clear evidence of this fact. Until we meet the need to direct and reinforce inner strengths, the flow of our energies may be misdirected or drained to a breaking point. When we feel physically and mentally tired, we operate less efficiently, and consequently live with insecurity, worry, tension, and anxiety. These circumstances, continued over a period of time, may manifest themselves in several ways—difficulty in falling asleep or getting restful sleep, moodiness, depression, and ultimately mental and emotional breakdown.

When we have control of our thoughts, we have mastered the technique of concentration, which allows us to focus our energy on one thing at a time and act decisively. Any drain on our energy reserves will disrupt our mental concentration. Perhaps one of the most damaging influences on our mental well-being is negative thinking. An imagined situation may evoke almost the same emotional response as a real one. When we dwell on imaginary problems or anticipate trouble of some sort, we create a threat to our well-being. Our bodies grow tense with anxiety and emotion. By turning from negative to positive thoughts, we ultimately control our emotional responses, saving energy for productive and pleasant situations.

Tension has been singled out by the American Medical Association as a major cause of heart attacks. Tension is the sensation and emotion you feel as a result of continuous mental and emotional stress, theoretically in response to a physical or psychological threat. The physiology of the body's response to tension and stress is as follows: "The body responds—or attempts to respond (barring disease or injury to vital organs)—to any type of stress in the same manner. Interpreting the stress as a call to action, it mobilizes itself through the interaction of the nervous and glandular systems which control the level of body activity. Adrenalins are secreted, stored energy is released, blood sugar level rises, and heart rate and blood pressure increase. When the stress is removed, calming hormones are released and the body returns to normal."[1] Using electromyography, we can measure the response of the muscles to various kinds of stress. *Muscular tension is always an accompanying symptom of general tension.* The next time you sense a feeling of pressure, indecisiveness, excitement, anger, or frustration, notice the tightness in your muscles.

Interestingly enough, you will also find that a release of muscular tension eases overall tension. By focusing the mind on the control and relaxation of muscular tension, we have a release mechanism for our entire system. Brief periods of relaxation bring us back mentally and emotionally refreshed. The cultivation and use of relaxation techniques and exercises are an effective

---

[1] Frank Vitale, *Individualized Fitness Program* (Englewood Cliffs, New Jersey: Prentice-Hall, Inc., 1973), p. 200.

method of obtaining relief from the build-up of tension. As with other types of exercise, you must practice relaxing in order to experience the benefits. The following exercises and techniques for relaxation are provided in the sincere hope that they will be practiced with real effort and concentration. Above all, you must teach your mind to master the art of relaxation and the process of easing tensions within the body.

EXERCISES

The following are exercises to use when you have the advantage of solitude, and a quiet place for a retreat. Music will help promote relaxation if it is soothing and quiet. Do not let your emotions or thought processes interfere with physical relaxation. Particularly in the beginning, the most important point of concentration should be your body.

1. Choose a particular time of day and make an effort to sit quietly for a few minutes each day at that time.

2. Sitting in a cross-legged position, rest your hands in your lap or on your knees. Gently close your eyes and concentrate on a single thing. Choose something that is pleasing for you to think about. Each time your mind is distracted, bring it back to your object of concentration.

3. Sitting quietly with your eyes closed, tighten your fists and mentally explore the feeling of tension within your hands. Slowly release the hands, studying the feeling of relaxation. Practice this several times until you are able to identify relaxation as it happens. Try this with different parts of your body.

4. Find a comfortable position lying on the floor. Try lying on your back, your head turned to one side, your arms away from your body, your feet and ankles loose. Turn your palms up and tighten your hands into a fist. Slowly let your hands relax. Concentrate on the feeling of relaxing your hands. Send the release up through your arms and relax the entire body.

5. Lying on the floor, roll to one side and curl up, bringing your knees to your chest. This is a position familiar to us as children. Turn your thoughts back to the day when you were young and life was full of adventure and curiosity. As you return to the present, bring back with you that sense of wonder and open your eyes to the adventures that lie ahead.

6. Find a position of relaxation. As you slowly close your eyes to the visual world around you, open your mind to experiencing the depths of your internal environment.

7. Sitting quietly or lying down, empty your mind of unhappy thoughts—anger, irritation, resentment, disappointment—and change to a positive outlook. Concentrate on being positive!

8. Think of yourself as a rag doll and collapse your body. Practice completely loosening every muscle you have.

9. Relax your mouth, lips, tongue, and throat. This is one method of turning off the constant words we turn over in our minds.

10. Practice releasing the muscles in the different areas of your face —cheeks, temples, lips, chin. Your face should be blank of all expression.

TECHNIQUES FOR HANDLING STRESS

Many stressful situations may confront us during our normal daily tasks. Here are a few techniques for handling such situations.

1.   Learn mental priority. Become aware of how rapidly and continuously your mind operates throughout the day. Periodically examine your thoughts, learning to sort out that which is worthwhile and that which is a waste of mental energy. Eliminate thoughts which are unnecessary and don't dwell on situations you can't change.

2.   Develop your own plans for handling hectic situations when they occur. Practice these and your reactions to such situations will be controlled and relaxed.

3.   When a bad situation does occur, resolve to handle it without emotion. That will drain your energies. Take a deep breath, gather your thoughts, and make a businesslike effort at resolving it.

4.   When you are the busiest, take a few moments to relax your thoughts and control preoccupation with your work. A brief retreat to a favorite spot or a quiet corner will keep tension under control and ultimately help you master your time.

In addition, we recommend recreational forms of physical and social activity as an enjoyable release. The list of possibilities is endless—learn to play tennis or golf, take a walk or a hike, try sailing or skin diving, enroll in a yoga class. Explore the possibilities and enjoy the pleasure—you've got a life to live!

There is a wealth of information available to help you master your time and your mind. The following books and articles are recommended as aids to your personal growth and mental well-being.

Recommended References

Books

Bahm, Archie J., *Yoga for Business Executives and Professional People*, New York: Citadel Press, 1965.

Hill, Napoleon, *Grow Rich! With Peace of Mind*, Grenwich, Connecticut: Fawcett Publication, Inc. (Fawcett Crest Books), 1967.

Hill, Napoleon and E. Harold Keown, *Succeed and Grow Rich Through Persuasion*, Grenwich, Connecticut: Fawcett Publication, Inc. (Fawcett Crest Books), 1970.

Hill, Napoleon, *Think and Grow Rich*, Grenwich, Connecticut: Fawcett Publication, Inc. (Fawcett Crest Books), 1960.

Hill, Napoleon, *You Can Work Your Own Miracles,* Grenwich, Connecticut: Fawcett Publication, Inc. (Fawcett Crest Books), 1971.

Hittleman, Richard, *Richard Hittleman's Guide to Yoga Meditation,* New York: Grosset and Dunlap, Inc. (Bantam Books), 1969.

Maltz, Maxwell, *Psycho-cybernetics and Self-Fulfillment,* New York: Grosset and Dunlap, Inc. (Bantam Books), 1970.

Peale, Norman Vincent, *Stay Alive All Your Life,* Grenwich, Connecticut: Fawcett Publication, Inc. (Fawcett Crest Books), 1957.

Peale, Norman Vincent, *The Power of Positive Thinking,* New York: Prentice-Hall, Inc., 1952.

Peterson, Wilfred A., *The Art of Living, Day By Day,* New York: Simon and Schuster, 1972.

Stevenson, George S., *Master Your Tensions and Enjoy Living Again,* Englewood Cliffs: Prentice-Hall, Inc., 1959.

Articles

Collier, James Lincoln, "Leisure—Why Don't We Enjoy It More?", *Reader's Digest,* July 1973.

Knight, Leavitt A., Jr., "How to Relax Without Pills", *Reader's Digest,* February 1971.

Ratcliff, J. D., "How to Avoid Harmful Stress", *Reader's Digest,* July 1970.

POSTLUDE

You've chosen a very difficult path to
travel . . . a path filled with opportunities
and disappointments, a path most people
try to avoid because of the responsibilities,
but I see you striving to push ahead and
I know you will succeed. You have chosen
the path to be real, and because of this
you will suffer, but you will grow.

— George Betts

By now you should have some idea of the effort it takes to maintain a good figure. Believe in yourself and you can handle the effort. You have the motivation, or you would not have come this far with us. And you have the knowledge you need. At this point, your job is to put that knowledge to work for you. You are preparing for the future and you should prepare well, for you are the one who has to live in your future.

Be positive: dispel negative thoughts, ideas, and words from your entire being and greet each day with enthusiasm now that you know how. Don't be discouraged by your mistakes; learn from them. Sometimes we will stumble and fall, but if we pick ourselves up and go forward again, we will succeed. Frustrations will confront you, but you need not worry now, for your outlook will get you past them; as the discipline begins to grow, the frustrations will diminish.

Make your figure and your health a lifetime concern. Be proud of the new you—the way you look, act and feel. Try to convince others that they, too, can change themselves, in body and mind. Remember, the successful woman is not afraid of hard work, and she accomplishes it with a sense of satisfaction and pride. Begin now to *create the new you!*

> We arrive in this world alone . . .
> Under the cover of the stars,
>> under the cover of the sun fermented into eternity
>> there lies a precious moment of time we call life.
> A gift of Creation.
> We are given minds to discover,
>> talent to create,
>> curiosity to gain knowledge,
>> insight to build,
>> emotions to communicate our feelings,
>> and movement through our physical body.
> Open your gift!
>
> — Walter Rinder

APPENDIX: CHARTS

CHART 1
ENERGY EXPENDITURE FOR VARIOUS ACTIVITIES

These values were established for persons weighing approximately 150 pounds. They should be increased or decreased proportionately to body weight by dividing your weight by 150 and multiplying the calories given on this chart by that number. For example, for a 125-pound woman, divide 125 by 150, which gives a coefficient of .83. Then multiply each calorie-per-hour figure by .83. Sitting, for example, would cost a 125-pound woman 83 calories instead of the given 100.

ACTIVITY	CALORIES PER HOUR	ACTIVITY	CALORIES PER HOUR
Rest and Light Activity	50-200		
Lying down or sleeping	80	Badminton (continuous play)	350
Sitting	100	Horseback riding (trotting)	350
Driving an automobile	120	Square dancing (continuous)	350
Standing	140	Volleyball (good players)	350
Domestic work	180	Roller skating	350
Moderate Activity	200-350	*Vigorous Activity*	350-900
Bicycling (5½ mph)	210	Table tennis (good players)	360
Walking (2½ mph)	210	Ditch digging (hand shovel)	400
Gardening	220	Ice skating (10 mph)	400
Canoeing (2½ mph)	230	Wood chopping or sawing	
Golf	250	by hand	400
Lawn mowing		Tennis (good players)	420
(power mower)	250	Water skiing	480
Fencing	300	Hill climbing (100 ft. per hr.)	490
Calisthenics		Squash and handball	600
(continuous movement)	300	Skiing	600
Rowing (2½ mph)	300	Cycling (13 mph)	660
Swimming (¼ mph)	300	Race rowing	840
Walking (3¾ mph)	300	Running (10 mph)	900

Source: Robert E. Johnson, M.D., Ph.D., and colleagues, Department of Physiology and Biophysics, University of Illinois, *Exercise and Weight Control* (Washington, D.C.: Committee on Exercise and Physical Fitness of the American Medical Association and the President's Council on Physical Fitness in cooperation with the Lifetime Sports Foundation), August 1967.

CHART 2
A POSTURE INVENTORY

AREA	NEED TO STRENGTHEN	NEED TO STRETCH	EXERCISES	NO.	PG.
Upper back and shoulders					
Along the spine					
Buttocks and hips					
Back of thigh					
Calf					
Chest					
Abdomen					
Front of thigh					

CHART 3
"IDEAL FIGURE" WEIGHT CHART

A Word About Weight Charts

Naturally, when you consult a height and weight chart, you assume it will tell you the appropriate weight for your height and bone structure. Before you accept a chart's "figures" as a guideline, however, you should be aware of the origin and significance of the statistics.

Unfortunately, most weight charts are based not on "ideal figures" but on statistical averages for a certain segment of the population. For example, the height and weight charts most commonly in use today are based on statistics compiled in 1959 by several insurance companies.[1] The records of these companies had shown that while an overweight person was a poor mortality risk, individuals who maintained their weight from age twenty-five on—whatever that weight might have been—had a lower death rate. Thus, the *average* height-weight figures for twenty-five-year-old men and twenty-five-year-old women as calculated on the basis of statistics provided by several million policyholders, were deemed "desirable." The haphazard method of arriving at these averages has been pointed out by Ronald Deutsch: "The authors of the charts assumed men's clothes to weigh from seven to nine pounds and women's from four to six. They allowed two inches for women's shoes and one inch for men's . . . The result was an average of the inaccurate weights and heights of people in three different body styles, with the builds judged by standards which scientists have pronounced of extremely limited significance. Ignored completely was the fact that a great number of the subjects were too fat, possibly a third of them markedly so."[2]

Thus even though your weight matches the weight recommended for you by most charts, you may well have to lose a few pounds more to obtain the figure you want. We have designed this "ideal figure" weight chart on the basis of the figures of fashion models, airline stewardesses, and—most importantly—the thousands of women with whom we have worked over the past twelve years. On the basis of that experience, we can say that the weight indicated on this chart for your height and body frame is likely to be very close to the weight at which you will achieve the figure you desire. As you look at this chart, remember that most weight charts in general use today are not based on slim-figure averages, but rather on the statistical averages for a whole generation of "fat Americans"!

---

[1] The following references contain a more detailed background of the weight charts from which this information was condensed:

Deutsch, Ronald M. *The Family Guide to Better Food and Better Health.* Des Moines, Iowa: Meredith Corporation (Better Homes and Gardens Creative Home Library), 1971.

Mayer, Jean. *Overweight: Causes, Cost, and Control.* Englewood Cliffs, N.J.: Prentice-Hall, 1968.

Solomon, Neil. *The Truth About Weight Control.* New York: Stein and Day, 1971.

Stuart, Richard B., and Davis, Barbara. *Slim Chance in a Fat World.* Champaign, Ill.: Research Press, 1972.

[2] Deutsch, *Family Guide to Better Food . . .*, p. 122.

How To Use the Chart

To determine your frame size, take your wrist measurement. (This is just a rule-of-thumb measure; it will not be accurate in all cases, so use your judgment as well.) Measure circumference just above the wrist bone (toward the elbow) on the arm that you least use.

Small Frame:	4 1/2" to 5 1/8"
Medium Frame:	5 3/8" to 6 1/8"
Large Frame:	6 1/4" to 6 3/4"

Next, measure your height accurately. If you fall between two heights shown, add one pound for each quarter inch. For example, if you are medium frame, 5'6½" tall, your ideal weight would be 122 pounds. In order to find your ideal weight range, add five pounds above and five pounds below your ideal weight as determined from the chart, so the weight range for the woman described above would be 117 to 127 pounds. You should always attempt to stay within your weight range. There are always a few exceptions to any standard. You might find that you must go five pounds or so above or below your range to achieve the results you desire.

Height	Small Frame	Medium Frame	Large Frame
4' 8"	65 lbs.	70 lbs.	75 lbs.
4' 9"	70	75	80
4' 10"	75	80	85
4' 11"	80	85	90
5' 0"	85	90	95
5' 1"	90	95	100
5' 2"	95	100	105
5' 3"	100	105	110
5' 4"	105	110	115
5' 5"	110	115	120
5' 6"	115	120	125
5' 7"	120	125	130
5' 8"	125	130	135
5' 9"	130	135	140
5' 10"	135	140	145
5' 11"	140	145	150
6' 0"	145	150	155
6' 1"	150	155	160
6' 2"	155	160	165

CHART 4
A STRENGTH EXERCISE PROGRAM

EXERCISE	NUMBER OF REPETITIONS								
	DATE								
1. Standing waist twist									
2. Arm fling									
3. Standing leg lift									
4. Side bend									
5. Sitting ankle flexion and extension									
6. Pop-ups									
7. Kneeling leg lift series									
8. Let-down									

CHART 5
A PROGRESSIVE RESISTANCE PROGRAM

PROGRAM _____	SETS _____	REPETITIONS _____								
		CHANGES								
EXERCISE	FOR	DATE								
1.										
2.										
3.										
4.										
5.										
6.										
7.										
8.										

This book was set in Theme Bold by Libra
Cold Type, and printed by National Press.
Sponsoring editor was C. Lansing Hays, editorial
supervisor was Carole Norton, and copy editor
was Gene Tanke. Michelle Hogan supervised
production. Illustrations were by Bob Carr
and Betty Clinton. Cover photograph was by
Michael Powers. Nancy Sears designed the
text and cover.